AF552541

Global Educational Studies

Global Educational Studies

Editor

Dr. DIGUMARTI BHASKARA RAO

M.Sc., M.A., M.A., M.Ed., Ph. D.

R.V.R. College of Education

Guntur

Andhra Pradesh

India

Discovery Publishing House

New Delhi

has been conceptualized as a fundamental right of all human beings and a goal in itself on the one hand, and as an essential means of action for pursuing development objectives in the perspective of sustainability on the other.

3. The demographic challenge to educations

If education is to provide in the longer term part of the policy response to population growth and other societal problems, in the short term the pressure of population growth on education systems remains the dominant issue in the developing countries.

Achieving universal basic education can represent very different challenges for different countries, depending on the national human and financial resources that can be mobilized as well as the rate of population growth and the age structure of the population.

In many parts of the developing world educational progress has been substantial...

In many parts of the developing world educational progress was substantial between 1970 and 1997. Estimated adult literacy rates in the world rose from 63 to 78 per cent during this period. World total enrolment at the primary level increased from 411 million in 1970 to 542 million in 1980, and to 668 million in 1997. This growth took place exclusively in the developing world where enrolment increased from 313 million in 1970 to 579 million in 1997[7].

...with primary enrolment now growing at almost double the pace than before Jomtien...

Between 1990 and 1997, primary education enrolment in all developing countries taken together grew by about 72 million pupils, almost double the pace observed during the 1980s. Net enrolment ratios also reflected a positive development, showing that growth in enrolment outpaced the growth of the primary school age population.

First Published-2001

Reprinted-2011

ISBN 81-7141-616-0

Published by :

Discovery Publishing House

4831/24, Ansari Road, Prahlad Street,

Darya Ganj, New Delhi-110002 (India)

☎ : 3279245 • Fax: 91-11-3253475

E-mail : dphtemp@indiatimes.com

Printed at:

Mehra Offset Press

Delhi

Preface

The EFA 2000 Assessment was planned to combine quantitative and qualitative information for a complete picture of progress in Education for All over the Jomtien decade. The 'expanded vision' saw basic education as comprising not only formal schooling but also literacy programmes, non-formal education-indeed, comprising all basic elements of an individual's lifelong education. To complement the EFA Country Reports, therefore, fourteen global thematic studies were commissioned. Their titles reflect some, though by no means all, of the key policy areas confronting basic educators in the first decade of the twenty-first century, no less than in the last decade of the twentieth. Their executive summaries appear in this book.

Within the overall framework of the EFA, Forum co-ordiantion of the research and writing of the studies was shared among various partners including DFID, SIDA, UNESCO, UNICEF, WHO, World Bank, and the NGO Consultative Forum. The process of consultation included consideration by participants in each of the Regional EFA Conferences which were held between December 1999 and February 2000.

These highly authoritative thematic studies provide rich insights and judgements about trends and issues that lie at the heart of the EFA movement. Each one provides theoretical vision and practical leadership to education planners and decision makers. Drawing on work being undertaken at the grassroots, each describes 'best practices' as well as successful and unsuccessful experiments in policy implementation.

UNESCO deserves the appreciation, special thanks are extended to the EFA Forum Secretariat and its personnel. This publication is the reproduction of material from EFA 2000 Assessment Thematic Studies—Executive Summaries published by UNESCO for consultation at the World Education Forum, Dakar, 2000.

D.B. Rao

International Literacy Day

Contents

Achieving Education for All: Demographic Challenges

The 1990 World Conference on Education for All in Jomtien reaffirmed the commitment of countries to meet basic learning needs of all children, youths and adults. Specific goals, in the light of which countries agreed to establish national targets, included universal access to and completion of basic education by the year 2000 and the reduction of adult illiteracy, with specific emphasis on eliminating gender disparities in educational opportunities. However, problems of economic stagnation, continued population growth, and economic and social disparities both among and within nations have posed various challenges to making this a reality.

1. Objectives

A decade has passed since Jomtien, What progress has been accomplished towards the goal of education for all? Is it possible to quantify the impact of demography on public policy, particularly on education? To what extent did policies directed towards universal access to primary education, the elimination of gender gaps and increasing net primary school enrolment ratios succeed in overcoming the challenges of population dynamics and resource constraints? Which policies have been the most effective and what can countries learn from the experience of others?

This paper examines what has been accomplished and what remains to be done, first from a global perspective and then with a focus on the less developed regions where the demographic transition is still underway and where universal basic education is still far from a really. Changes in enrolment ratios, literacy rates, gender disparities, public investment in education, as well as shortages in educational provision and inadequate conditions of learning are considered against the backdrop of demographic changes. Regional figures, however, hide considerable variations within regions and even within countries, masking important differences in policies. In order to detect these variations, the situation of individual countries is presented for some specific issues. The relative success of national policies in meeting EFA goals is also examined through a comparison of the E-9 countries that together account for more than half of the world's population (Bangladesh, Brazil, China, Egypt, India, Indonesia, Mexico, Nigeria and Pakistan).

Specifically, the paper:

- Describes population growth at the world and regional level, and summarises the recent international debate on population, development and education with a focus on the impact of education on population dynamics;
- Examines the impact of demographic growth on the achievement of education for all in the less developed regions of the world, outlining different policy approaches adopted in pursuing the goal of education for all against the demographic pressure.
- Quantifies how E-9 countries have progressed towards universal primary education and the effort needed to fill the remaining gap by 2010 in terms of additional students to enrol, using different enrolment benchmarks;
- Highlights some of the challenges ahead and the main priorities for action towards the achievement of education for all from the perspective of population and sustainable development.

2. The role of education in the context of population growth and development

The world population has grown rapidly...

During the last forty years, the world population doubled, leading to a figure of 6 billion in 1999. By the middle of the next century, the world population is projected to grow further to between 7.3 and 10.7 billion, with 8.9 billion considered the most likely estimate. About half of the world's citizens are currently under the age of 24.

While fertility declined in all regions of the world, except sub-Saharan Africa, from a global total of over 5 births per women in 1950 to an estimated 2.7 births at present, the young age structure of the world population still implies a growth of 78 million per year. Another thirty to forty years will have to pass, according to the scenario based on medium fertility assumptions, before the annual population increment falls back to the size of 1950.

Even more significant than the rate of growth or the magnitude of the numbers involved, is the fact that ninety-seven per cent of the world population increase occurs in the less developed regions of the world. Every year the population of Asia is increasing by 50 million, the population of Africa by 17 million and that of Latin America and the Caribbean by nearly 8 million.[1]

..but so has the world economy.

Demographic growth must not be seen in isolation. In general, it is where population growth outpaces economic growth, and thus gross national product (GNP) per capita declines and where population growth reinforces social and economic disparities that pressure on economic stability and social cohesion may occur.

Economic growth and wealth creation in the past century were both spectacular. While over the three centuries from 1500 to 1820, world GDP roughly tripled, during the 170 years after 1820 it increased more than 40-fold. Against this background, the world population growth seems modest[2]. However, there has been much less success in distributing wealth than in creating it, not just across countries but also within them, creating new imbalances and further problems to be faced.

There is no general pattern in the relationship between population and development...

Whether rapid population growth influences the pace of economic development or indeed whether it is the pace of economic development that influences the rate of population growth, is a question that continues to attract the attention of the scientific and popular debate. For many years, empirical studies have failed to find evidence of strong or consistent relationships, either positive or negative, between demographic change and subsequent economic growth. Causal links and inter-relationships between population and development are complex, and as they also differ between countries, it is difficult to identify general patterns. Furthermore, the level of economic development that a country achieved prior to the onset of rapid population growth has an impact on the consequences of that growth: in general, the more advanced the level of development, the less the impact of population growth[3].

...although in developing countries slower population growth seems to be beneficial to economic development.

Analytical and empirical findings seem to support the conclusion that on balance, slower population growth would be beneficial to economic development for most developing countries. Moreover, recent analyses, based on data since the end of the 1970s, have revealed fairly large negative association between rapid population growth and growth rates of per capita output[4]. Lately, the predominant view is that slower rates of population growth can buy more time to adjust and can increase countries ability to attack poverty, protect and repair the environment, and build the base for future sustainable development[5].

How do demographic and economic trends interact in different countries?

It is instructive to examine the way in which demographic and economic trends developed and interacted in different countries. In general, in countries such as Pakistan and Nigeria, where fertility rates remain high, economic growth and wealth per capita cannot afford the annual expansion of the population at its current level. Conversely, countries such as China, Indonesia, Brazil, and Egypt, where the population is growing at slower rates and the demographic transition is underway, benefit from increasing rates of economic growth and present an increased wealth per capita. Although any conclusion is preliminary, the evidence presented seems to show, for the E-9 countries, a negative association between rapid population growth and growth rates of per capita output.

Rising levels of education play an important role in accelerating the pace of transition.

Concern with rapid population growth has led researches and policy-makers to examine the determinants of fertility change. In particular, increased participation of women in education has proved to have an important impact on reducing material, infant and child mortality, to be consistently associated with lower fertility and to contribute to gender equality[6].

The Jomtien conference, as well as most of the education and development conferences held in the 1990s, underlined the certrality of education, recognising its role and benefits in combating poverty, empowering women, promoting human rights and democracy, protecting the environment and controlling population growth. In this perspective, education

The number of out-of-school children of the official primary school age groups was 95 million in 1990 and was expected to decline further to 88 million in 2000 and 79 million in 2010[8]. In particular, the number of out-of-school children decreased in Eastern Asia and Oceania and to a lesser extent in Latin America and the Caribbean.

...but in some regions, a growing minority continues to be left out.

Conversely, in sub-Saharan Africa, the Arab States and somewhat less in Southern Asia the achievement of universal primary education has been hindered by the growth and age-structure of populations. Efforts to increase primary enrolment ratios have had to work against a rapidly growing population. Thus, despite significant growth in enrolment, the number of out-of-school children did not decline correspondingly.

Different policy strategies have adopted in order to expand access to schooling.

Many countries in all of the less developed regions organised national policy meetings on Education for All in the early 1990s and several of them adopted EFA policies and plans. Policy strategies aimed at favouring the expansion of access to schooling included a movement of decentralisation of the management of education institutions as well as, in some cases, of curricula; the building of new partnerships and a more marked involvement of the community; the introduction of instruction in the mother tongue; the diversification of schooling and the promotion of programmes for dropout children; the sensitisation of parents to the value of education; and the institution of free primary education.

Primary education will no longer suffice to meet demands of tomorrow's societies...

If the completion of primary education enables people to take care of their own and their family's hygiene, nutrition and health, further education is required in order to participate effectively in today's knowledge-based economies and societies. The number of enrolled young people of secondary school-age grew by about 83 million throughout the world between 1990 and 1997, of which 74 million were in developing countries. Positive trends in net enrolment ratios during the 1990s confirm that in general enrolment of secondary school age youth grew faster than the relevant age population. In some countries, however, more than half of the pupils of secondary school age were enrolled in primary school, as repeaters or late entrants.

...although in the less developed regions it still represents the only educational opportunity for the majority.

Overall, the proportion of the official school-age population actually enrolled in secondary education continues to be low. In the year 2000 it was estimated to be higher than 50 per cent only in Eastern Asia and Oceasnia (55 per cent) and the Arab States (51 per cent). In Latin America and the Caribbean, and in Southern Asia only 44 and 43 per cent respectively of the official school-age population was enrolled in secondary school. In sub-Saharan Africa the proportion enrolled in secondary education was only 24 per cent and in the least developed countries taken together, only 18 per cent. Primary education remains therefore the only educational opportunity for more than 80 per cent of the school-age population in the least developed countries, for more than 75 per cent in sub-Saharan Africa, and for 45 to 57 per cent in the other developing regions. It is therefore crucial that primary education be able to answer the basic learning needs of tomorrow's adults.

Illiteracy declined in developing regions, but not at the desired pace...

Levels of literacy within a population are an indicator of the human potential that can promote the social, economic and cultural development of a country and many studies have confirmed that throughout the world the best predictor of the learning achievement of children is the education and literacy level of their parents.

The estimated number of literate adults aged 15 years and over went from 2.7 billion people in 1990 to 3.4 billion in 2000, that is, from 75 to 79 per cent of the world's adult population. If illiteracy rates decreased in all of the less developed regions, this decline did not progress at the desired pace and efforts of governments had to work against the obstacle of an ever increasing population. In the least developed countries taken together, one adult in two is still illiterate, that is, lacks the basic reading, writing and numeracy skills essential to develop and function at both the individual and societal level. In the year 2000, among the less developed regions, the problem of illiteracy seems to be particularly serious in Southern Asia, sub-Saharan Africa and the Arab States, with estimated percentages of illiterates of 46, 40 and 39 per cent respectively.

... and gender disparities in access to educational opportunities are still large.

The mid-decade meeting of the Forum on Education for All held in Amman in 1996 judged insufficient the progress achieved in closing the gender gap during the 1990s and reaffirmed the education of girls and women as 'the priority of priorities'. The share of girls in the primary school age out-of-school population decreased by only one percentage point during the 1990s, from 60 to 59 per cent. In the least developed countries considered alone, the proportion of primary school age out-of-school girls increased even, from 54 to 56 per cent. At the regional level, the disparities were more pronounced in Southern Asia and sub-Saharan Africa, where female enrolment ratios would have to increase by 12 and 9 percentage points, respectively, in order to attain gender equality. The regional averages, however, hid marked differences across countries. For example, in the African region south of the Sahara, countries where the enrolment of girls is some 25 percentage points lower than that of boys, such as Benin and Chad, co-exist with countries where the gender gap penalizes boys, such as Botswana and Lesotho.

Similarly, women's access to educational resources remains inadequate in a large part of the developing world. It was estimated that in 1990 there were 322 million illiterate men and 560 million illiterate women (i.e. over 30 per cent of the adult female population) in the world. In 2000, the percentage of illiterate women was estimated to be 26.4, and the gender gap will have decreased slightly (from 13.3 percentage points in 1990 in 11.7 in 2000).

The educational disadvantage of women is only one aspect of the discrimination from which they suffer in many countries where women are the poorest of the poor. In order to succeed in closing the gender gap in educational opportunities, against the obstacles posed by poverty and demographic pressure, priorities and commitment of government would have to be directed at the heart of the problem—overcoming the tendency to devalue women. This implies not only using all means to improve access to and participation of girls and women in education but also conveying through the contents and methods of that education the value of women and an egalitarian view of human beings.

Progress in expanding enrolment has not always been matched by increases in the quality of educational provision as it can be seen from survival rates to Grade 5...

What matters, ultimately, is not just the volume of participation in education but more importantly—and as stressed in the World Declaration on Education for All—what people actually learn as a result of participating in education. This, in turn, depends on the quality of education. One indicator of quality that is often used is the percentage of a pupil cohort reaching Grade 5. In general, the school experience of many children in the developing world is relatively brief and unsatisfactory. In Southern Asia, Latin America and the Caribbean, and sub-Saharan Africa, it is estimated that less than three out of four pupils reach Grade 5. In the least developed countries taken together, only half of the pupils reach this grade level. Indeed, many students drop out between the first and the second grade, having acquired not even the most basic elements of an education. This probably reflects both the poverty of these children and their families, and the inability of schools to respond adequately to their needs.

...the conditions of school equipment and supplies...

Many experts have expressed concern over the conditions of learning in over-crowded schools of the developing world, and their impact upon achievement. Based on the responses of school-heads in a pilot survey of conditions of learning in the least developed countries conducted in 1995, it appeared that between the Jomtien Conference and 1995, the volume of school equipment and supplies had either remained constant or decreased, which means that, given the general increase in enrolments, the conditions of primary schools had deteriorated overall.

... pupils-teacher ratios...

The expansion of enrolment during the first EFA decade made the chronic shortage of qualified teachers more critical. In the less developed regions taken together, pupil-teacher ratios were twice as large as those in the more developed ones, while in the least developed countries they were three times as large. A high pupil-teacher ratio can initially by one means for keeping costs low while expanding enrolment. However, high pupil-teacher ratios, combined with inadequate instructional equipment and low teacher motivation cannot contribute to learning.

... as well as from investment and spending patterns in education...

Investment in education is a key determinant of the scope, quality and impact of education in a country. Expenditure on education can be used as an indicator to assess the implementation of EFA targets. While public current expenditure rose in all developing regions except in Southern Asia, enrolments also increased. The result was that the additional investment did not always lead to an increase in resources available per pupil. In fact, at the pre-primary and primary level the public current expenditure per pupil as a percentage of GNP per capita decreased in sub-Saharan Africa and in Southern Asia. Thus, in these two regions it seems that a trade-off was made after Jomtien to enrol more students at a lower cost. On the other hand, in Latin America, and Eastern Asia and Oceania, along with expansion of the enrolled school age population, the expenditure per student also increased.

Among the policy measures common to various countries that have achieved universal primary education early in their development process is the allocation of a higher expenditure per pupil as a percentage of GNP per capita into primary education and a lower one into higher education compared with other countries in the same regions[9].

One of the necessary responses to the problems the scarcity of resources is a clear commitment to giving high macro-economic priority to education, together with health and other basic social services, and to re-examining—according to the suggestion of the Jomtien Declaration and Framework for Action, and the successful examples of countries which can be considered as high-achievers— spending patterns and unit costs at the different levels of the education system in order to allocate higher shares of education budgets to basic education.

4. A closer look at half of the world population

In all E-9 countries, the number of enrolled primary-school-age children rose between 1990 and 1997 and the increase exceeded the corresponding change in the number of primary-school-age children in the population, thus indicating that educational progress outpaced demographic growth. Countries, however, varied in their pace of change. The following analysis is based on the 1999 provisional and estimates and projections of the UNESCO Institute for Statistics. However, given the weakness in many of the data on which estimates and projections are based, the results should be interpreted as broad trends and used with caution.

Some countries achieved or are close to achieving universal primary education...

In China, Indonesia, Brazil, Mexico and Egypt, the increase of primary-school-age enrolments, representing a main goal of national policies, accompanied by a decline of the primary-school-age population, implies that universal primary education will be achieved by 2010 (or shortly after in the case of Egypt). In China, the sharp decline of the primary-school-age population, by more than 30 million pupils in just 10 years, was one of the factors that permitted the provision of a place in school to every child by 1990. In Indonesia, the growth in primary-school-age enrolments outpaced the growth of the primary-school-age population between 1980 and 1990 and practically all primary-school-age children had the opportunity to participate in education at some point during the 1980s. In Brazil, the 1990s marked the turning point in the growth of their primary-school-age population. The decrease in the number of children, coupled with a policy aimed at increasing enrolment ratios in primary school is predicted to result in the achievement of universal primary education by the year 2000. In Mexico, universal primary education was already achieved by 1980, so that a moderate expansion of the number of primary school age children during the 1990s was easily covered by a corresponding expansion of enrolment. In Egypt, the growth in the number of enrolments outpaced the growth in the number of primary-school-age children during the 1980s and 1990s, and it is estimated that the number of out-of-school children declined by more than 80 per cent between 1980 and 200. The expansion of the primary-school-age population is projected to stop in 2000, which will facilitate the achievement of universal primary education during the first decade of the twenty-first century.

...while the challenge remains to improve learning conditions and achievements.

In such countries the challenge is now to improve learning conditions and achievement, increase the internal efficiency of education systems, reduce school disparities in educational outcomes and expand participation in education beyond primary school.

In other countries, the expansion of primary enrolment was partially offset by the growth of the youth population.

In India, Pakistan, Bangladesh and Nigeria the expansion of primary-school-age enrolments supported by national policies was partially offset by the increase of the primary-school-age population so that, based on current trends, the achievement of universal primary education lies in the future, at some point after 2010. In India, primary-school-age enrolments rose but so did the primary-school-age population, which increased up to 2000 when it is projected to stabilise, thus leading to only a slight decrease of the out-of-school population. Based on the trends obtained from available statistics, it is predicted that the number of enrolled primary-school-age children will not change significantly during the first decade of the twenty-first century, with the result that 20 million children could still be out-of-school in the year 2010. In Pakistan, as in India, rapid population growth remains a challenge to achieving universal primary education, countering as it does a continuing expansion of primary-school-age enrolments. The number of out-of-school children decreased steadily during the 1990s, while enrolment underwent a remarkable growth in this post-Jomtien decade. However, unlike in India, the primary-school-age population is expected to continue expanding in the first decade of the twenty-first century, so that additional resources will serve mainly to keep abreast of population growth, and the process of educational recovery will proceed at a slow pace. In Bangladesh, some progress was made during the 1990s in increasing primary-school-age enrolment ratios, after primary education was made compulsory in 1993. The number of primary-school-age enrolled children is predicted to increase by 3 million, between 2000 and 210, while the number of out-of-school children is expected to decrease by just 1 million during the same period, due to a new expansion of the primary school age children cohorts. Finally, in Nigeria, by 2010 there will be twice as many primary-school-age children than there were in 1980, given that there are no signs of a decline in demographic growth. Student demography thus offsets the considerable efforts made to increase the number of enrolled children, which are particularly evident after 1990. Without an inversion of this demographic trend it will take many more years to find a place in school for the 20 per cent of primary school age children that are currently excluded from it.

Four benchmarks are used to quantify the efforts needed to achieve universal primary education.

In order to quantify the efforts needed in the E-9 countries that have not yet enrolled all of their primary-school-age children, four benchmarks have been used in the paper: universal enrolment, net enrolment ratios of 90 per cent, the net enrolment ratio in less developed regions in 2000 (84.8 per cent), and a scenario in which the current rates of progress will prevail.

Based on the 1999 provisional estimates and projections of the UNESCO Institute for Statistics, Pakistan, Nigeria and Bangladesh will be required to increase their enrolment by 32 per cent, 26 per cent and 25 per cent respectively, if they are to reach by 2010 the estimated net enrolment ratio of the less developed regions in the year 2000. These percentage increases correspond to enrolling 5 million more primary-school-age children in Pakistan, 3.8 million more in Nigeria and 2.7 million more in Bangladesh. India will need to enrol more than 2 million additional children.

In order to achieve 90 per cent net enrolment ratios by 2010, India will be required to increase its enrolment by about

9 per cent, enrolling 8 million additional primary-school-age children. Pakistan, Nigeria and Bangladesh are required to expand their enrolments by between 33 and 40 per cent, with respect to the level each country had reached in the year 2000.

Finally, the ideal universal enrolment scenario implies a growth in enrolment ratios that estimated to range from 5 per cent in Egypt to 55 per cent in Pakistan, with respect to the current situation of each country. The percentage increases required to achieve universal primary education correspond to enrolling almost half a million primary-school-age children more than in 2000 in Egypt, 5 million more in Bangladesh, 7 million more in Nigeria, almost 9 million more in Pakistan and 19 million more in India. Based on these figures, the universal enrolment scenario seems to be difficult to reach for these countries by 2010, unless major efforts are made and additional resources are mobilised to increase the rate of educational progress.

The situation of the E-9 countries reflects that of the other developing countries. In 2000, of the 107 developing countries for which estimates were available, 32 had achieved net enrolment ratios of more than 95 per cent, another 28 between 80 and 95 per cent while 47 countries were below the 80 per cent mark, with 15 countries having less than half of the official primary-school-age population enrolled in school.

5. Main priorities and open challenges ahead

It is important to acknowledge the efforts that have been made during these ten years by many national governments, multilateral and bilateral organisation, and non-governmental organisations, as well as individuals, including local policy-makers, teachers and parents. Thanks to these efforts, the targets seem more easily attainable today than was the case ten years ago. Recognising such progress however, should not lead to a slowing down of the pace of the educational recovery, since the achievement of education for all still lies ahead.

Enrolment targets should be harmonised with the attainment of sufficient quality standards.

In order to enable all countries to achieve universal primary education without sacrificing the quality of the teaching/learning experience, countries starting from different points of departure may have to establish different intermediate national targets, combining the common urge with realistic timeframes. In order to harmonise quantity, that is the expansion of enrolment, with quality, that is achievement, the minimum sufficient standards to be attained need to be defined, measured and guaranteed, while progressively expanding enrolment.

Reliable and timely data on learning outcomes are needed.

More research is needed on learning achievement, in order to be able to assess, monitor and guide the progress towards the universal acquisition of basic literacy and numeracy skills, as well as 'life skills'. Efforts and progresses have been made in this direction. At least fifty nations carry out national assessments of learning achievement (International Consultative Forum on Education for All, forthcoming). The International Association for the Evaluation of Educational Achievement (IEA) has carried out numerous international assessments over the last 40 years[10]. Although some developing countries participated in these studies, however, it was mainly developed countries that were involved. Conversely, in recent years, a number of international assessment projects have been undertaken with the aim of involving developing countries, proving also for them both the feasibility and utility of this type of exercise[11].

The remaining gaps should be targeted sharing successful initiatives and policies.

Renewed efforts will be required to reach the child population that is still out-of-school bearing in mind that progress may now require greater efforts than those required previously, given that those that are not in school yet are likely to be the most difficult to reach for different reasons.

Although much has been done to promote the participation of girls and women in education, innovative experiences have to be shared and multiplied in order to overcome continued discrimination against girls and women and fully address gender issues.

Also in the area of adolescents' and adults' literacy and education, countries could benefit from an exchange of information and experiences involving intergovernmental and non-governmental organisations, associations and private partners.

Macro-economic priority should reflect the importance of primary education.

Funding schemes should reflect the highest priority of primary education given that in the developing world this represents the only educational opportunity for a share of the child population that ranges from 45 to 80 per cent depending on the region and that it has proved to have a powerful impact on health care, reproductive and social behaviours which are at the core of sustainable development.

The spirit and goal of education for all should be shared by the whole society.

Schooling risks to fail its mission if it educates according to values and visions that are not supported, shared and conveyed by the society as a whole. Reforming education implies therefore a parallel process at the societal level with the aim of constantly instilling the vision of education for all and its goals into the minds of the world's societies.

International co-operation should mark a shift from a global towards a more united world.

Education for all represents a challenge for all regions of the world, with the poorest and most populous countries requiring particular attention and support also by the international community. Agreeing that education for all calls out for a response from the 'world as a whole' means going beyond the simple acknowledgment that we live in a global world. 'Global' does not necessarily means safe, good for everyone or harmonic. It simply points at the inter-dependence among the parts so that what happens in one part of the globe may have repercussions on what happens in several other parts.

Globalisation, however, provides the opportunity to direct the chain of interdependent actions and reactions towards progress for all human beings. The responsible and ethical management of globalization may contribute to a more co-operative and united world.

Notes:

1. *United Nations. World Population Prospects.* The 1998 Revision. New York. Department of Economic and Social Affairs, Population Division, United Nations, 1999

2. OECD. *Building Momentum for Global Growth and Social Progress into the new Millennium,* Note by the Secretary-General, Council at Ministerial Level, 26-27 May 1999.

3. United Nations. *Population Growth and Demographic Structure,* New York. Department of Economic and Social Affairs, Population Division, United Nations, 1999

4. D. Blanchet. "Reversal of the Effects of Population Growth on Economic Growth since the End of the 1970s: Reality or artefact?" In: *World Population Prospects,* op. cit. United Nations.

5. United Nations, *Reviews and Appraisal of the Progress Made in Achieving the Goals and Objectives of the Programme of Action of the International Conference on Population and Development,* New York. Department of Economic and Social Affairs, Population Division, 1999.

6. United Nations. *The World's Women 1995: Trends and Statistics,* New York, United Nations, 1995; United Nations. *World Population Monitoring 1996.* New York, Department of Economic and Social Affairs, Population Division, United Nations, 1998.
7. UNESCO, *Statistical Yearbook 1999,* Paris, UNESCO Publishing, 1999.
8. UNESCO Institute for Statistics, 1999 estimates and projections.
9. S. Mehrotra. Education for All: Policy Lessons from High-Achieving Countries, New York, UNICEF, 1998.
10. The latest IEA projects include the Reading Literacy Study, whose results were published in 1994 and the Third International Mathematics and Science Study (TIMSS), whose results were published in 1996 and 1997.
11. Such projects include the Southern African Consortium for Measuring Educational Quality (SACMEQ) undertaken by Ministries of Education in co-operation with the International Institute for Educational Planning (IIEP) of UNESCO, the Monitoring Learning Achievement (MLA)-project sponsored by UNESCO and UNICEF, the Programme of Analysis of Educational System (PASEC) established by the Ministries of Education of French-speaking countries in sub-Saharan Africa, and the Latin American Laboratory for Assessment of Educational Quality (Laboratorio), sponsored by UNESCO. For more information on the assessment of learning achievement, see International Consultative Forum on Education for All, Assessing Learning Achievement, forthcoming.

◆◆◆

2

Applying New Technologies and Cost-Effective Delivery Systems in Basic Education

There are three starting assumptions for a review of the use of information and communication technologies to support basic education. First, there is no practical substitute for primary schools so that the role of the technologies is to support primary education, not to replace it. Second, the technologies may, however, play a part in meeting the needs of children or adults who cannot get to school or conventional class. Third, it makes sense to look at the technologies together, from print to broadcasting to computers.

1. Definitions

We have used the following working definitions:

Telematics is the combined use of telecommunication and computer technology. *New information technologies, and information and communication technologies*, are synonyms for telematics.

Distance education is an educational process in which a significant proportion of the teaching is conducted by someone removed in space and/or time from the learner.

> *Open learning* is an organised educational activity, based on the use of teaching materials, in which constraints on study are minimised in terms either of access, or of time and place, pace, method of study, or any combination of these.
>
> *Open and distance learning* is an umbrella term covering distance education, open learning, and the use of telematics in education.
>
> *Computer-based learning* is the use of computers in education either to provide programmes that deliver instruction, or to facilitate communication between learner and tutor, or to enable students to have access to remote sources of information.

It is useful to distinguish between a variety of different applications of the various technologies to basic education. Computers have been used within schools both to support teaching and for school linking. Radio and television have been used in various formats for education within school. Open and distance learning has been used for two main purposes: to offer an out-of-school alternative to junior secondary education and for teacher education, where computer technologies are also beginning to be used. Broadcasting, and other technologies, have been widely used for the non-formal education of adults.

2. The position in 1990

At the time of the Jomtien conference it was argued that the potential of the new communication technologies had not been fully realised although there was, by that date, well-documented experience of their use for a range of educational purposes. This included the work of out-of-school institutions, notably in Latin America, which were providing an alternative to formal schooling; the use of radio and television to raise school quality; the use of radio, with other technologies, for adult education and extension; and teacher education through open and distance learning. At that time some open universities, notably in Asia, were beginning to work in basic education; computers were coming into classrooms in the north; the two new specialised agencies, the Commonwealth of Learning and the *Centre International Francophone de Formation a Distance,* were beginning to promote international cooperation in and through distance education.

3. The present environment and the last decade

Educational expansion and constraint over the last decade form the backdrop to any examination of the role of technology. The constraints on expansion mean that there remain large numbers of children outside school, especially in sub-Saharan Africa and south Asia, and large numbers of adults who missed schooling. One remarkable and consistent pattern is important: that, in all parts of the developing world, female enrolment in education, at primary secondary and tertiary levels, has been growing faster than male.

The environment within which technologies are applied to education has also been changing. The process towards digitisation has brought a convergence between different media and technologies. School and colleges all round the world have begun to use the Internet. At the same time, the process has been far from uniform and there is a widening gap between those with, and without, access to computer-based technologies. In many parts of the world, communications have also been deregulated and privatised, offering new kinds of access to communication technology but sometimes reducing the free access previously enjoyed by educators. Within the world of development communication there has been a new emphasis on participatory methodologies which has affected programmes of basic education, especially in out-of-school settings. One significant change in the formal sector has been the new legitimacy of open and distance learning, marked by the establishment of open universities in many countries but affecting education at all levels.

4. Technologies

Despite and convergence between technologies, it is convenient to distinguish between the various uses of computers, broadcasting and distance education.

Computers have been used in the classroom for five different reasons: to build up a workforce with skills in information technology; to educate all future citizens about the technologies; to change the curriculum often by using computer-assisted learning; to promote change in education; to give access to the Internet and e-mail. The last of these has achieved particular prominence and attention in the last few years. The choice of rationale determines the level in the education system at which it is appropriate to invest in telematics. All rationales demand adequate investment in staff training ad in software, both often under-emphasised in early planning. Whereas industrialised countries are moving towards the provision of computers to all classrooms, alternative strategies for providing computer access include the use of mobile units, the sharing of computer facilities with other agencies and mediated access where a third party seeks information through computer networks on behalf of a school.

Broadcasting has been used to offer direct teaching in schools, to provide enrichment programmes, and for general children's programming. One variant of direct teaching, interactive radio instruction, has been widely adopted, most often with funding support from the United States Agency for International Development (USAID).

Distance education, which is likely to rely on other technologies, print, broadcasts, and now sometimes computers, is being used for two main purposes in basic education: to offer an alternative form of junior-secondary, and more rarely primary education, and to support teacher education.

5. Audiences

Technologies have been used in school, mainly to raise quality, for out-of-school adolescents and adults, and for the in-service training and updating of intermediaries such as teachers and extension agents.

In school much attention has recently been given to the use of computers. Some computer projects have been designed as part of a programme of curriculum development. Increasingly, attention has gone to providing access to resources through the Internet, the development of skills in using the Internet and school-linking projects in which e-mail or computer conferencing techniques are used for school-to-school exchange. As these developments have add-on costs they increase the total cost per student.

Broadcasting has not been eclipsed by computers, and both television and radio continue to be used in schools. A series of interactive radio instruction projects, in which students are active in the classroom, responding to the radio teacher, have been run in many parts of the world. The projects have been successful in increasing student learning. Interactive radio demands heavy investment in curriculum development and its costs mean that the projects have not always been sustainable once initial donor funding has been withdrawn.

Various communication technologies have been used for audiences outside school. The unsatisfied demand for junior secondary education has led to a number of open and distance learning programmes. Telesecundaria in Mexico is a television-based, rural system offering secondary education which has been running for more than a quarter century and is a regular part of the national system of education. In Asia, open schools, relying more heavily on printed materials, have been established, notably in India and Indonesia, and have plans for large-scale expansion. Education out of school is not limited to the formal curriculum and also includes community-based educational projects, some of the beginning to use small-scale community radio, health campaigns and a wide range of projects for adult basic education. Some have used group study; many have been supported and organised by non-governmental organisations (NGOs). Many have worked well with small audiences but have had difficulty in moving to scale or establishing the links government agencies that would be necessary for this kind of expansion. The establishment of telecentres, open access centres at which, for a fee, individuals can get access to computer technologies and use the Internet, may provide new opportunities for informal and non-formal education.

The new technologies have been used in various ways to meet the needs of deprived and marginalised children, from those in remote areas to street children, refugees and war victims. Within industrialised countries Internet-based approaches have been used to meet the educational needs of migrant children. Radio and distance education have been used for the education of refugees. Broadcasting has been used for children in war zones on, for example, the hazards of land mines and to provide health education.

A variety of technologies have been used to provide in-service education and training for teachers, and to a lesser extent for agricultural and health extension agents. Some programmes are designed to make resources available to teachers, without a formal teaching structure. In other cases formal programmes have been run, in most parts of the world, using distance education for teachers. Programmes have usually engendered high motivation, especially where linked with improved qualifications and increased pay. Distance education for teacher training has proved to be effective, both in terms of examination pass rates and in raising teachers' capacities in the classroom.

6. Outcomes and costs

Outcomes may be assessed in terms of widening access, of improving quality or of changing the curriculum. In principle the use of mass media should widen access and there are examples of alternative systems of education that reach students who would otherwise be deprived of education. At the same time, the use of information and communication technologies may have the opposite effect, allowing the privileged access to learning through computer technology that is denied to others. There is evidence of qualitative improvement from programmes using distance education for teacher training and from the use of broadcasts in the classroom. Projects using both broadcasts and computers have been successful in helping a process of curriculum change. We have, however, few evaluations of the use of computers in the classroom, even from industralised countries with significant national investment.

Comparison between the costs of conventional and technology-based education is necessarily complex. The balance between fixed and variable costs is different in these two sectors. Economies of scale may be achieved in broadcasting or distance education so that, to determine the unit cost of a programme, we need to know the number of students. At the same time many uses of technology demand elements of individual support to which these economies do not apply. Programmes to raise the quality of education generally increase costs: they are not usually designed to reduce conventional staffing so that the costs of providing broadcasts or introducing computers are normally additional to regular educational costs.

Differing levels of salary make international comparison of costs difficult but, for what it is worth, evidence from a number of countries suggests that interactive radio annual costs per student are likely to be in the range \$3 to \$8, for student numbers in the range of 100,000 to 1,000,000. A small number of studies of the costs of computers in schools, where cconomies of scale are unlikely to apply, are several times as great, with figures in the range \$18 to \$ 63. The evidence is consistent in showing that television has higher costs than radio, sometimes ten times as high, and that computer-based learning is likely to have markedly higher costs than radio. Out-of-school distance-education projects have compared favourably in cost per student with conventional schooling; only if their success rate is adequately high do their costs per successful student compare favourably. The limited data available on adult basic education suggest that the costs compare favourably with face-to-face education for adults but are usually significantly higher, if measured in cost per learning hour, than the costs of primary education. In-service education of teachers using distance-teaching methods has often cost only between one-third and two-third that using the methods of conventional teacher education.

7. Conditions for success

The evidence, from television to computers, is that projects are likely to be at risk if they are at the leading edge of technology; education is likely to do better, in terms of costs and servicing of equipment, if it follows rather than leads entertainment and commerce. If technological innovation is to be sustainable it needs to generate a sense of ownership among all the stake-holders. Innovation is also likely to need an organisational location that allows adequate freedom for the innovator while remaining close enough to the work of conventional education and its decision-makers for it to achieve integration with the regular education service.

Many innovative projects have suffered from under-investment in training and in software, whether in the form of radio scripts or computer software. Training is generally needed both for specialists involved in the development of teaching materials and for teachers who are using them in their schools or adult educators or extension agents in the field.

8. Funding

The application and level of cost of new technologies is likely to lead to a search for new sources of funding. Where new technologies increase costs, there is likely to be tension between attempts to take advantage of their capacity to widen access and the search for ways of funding them: access may be possible at a price that only the more privileged can pay. One consequence of adopting telematics may be to shift responsibility for funding from the teaching institution to the learner, or from a central institution to an individual school or college. Downloading materials electronically, rather than buying them commercially or receiving, rather than buying them commercially or receiving them through a ministry of education, shifts the location of costs and may in fact increase them. At the same time, it may sometimes be possible to locate community funds by decentralising.

Many technology projects have been launched with external funding. Often this has excluded recurrent costs and led to problems of sustainability when neither learners nor governments are able to meet running costs.

The funding of out-of-school education has often been on a different basis from in-school education. Students outside school, often politically powerless, are frequently asked to pay a higher proportion of the costs of their education than those in school, sometimes in the expectation that they will be earning while studying. This means that those who receive what they perceive as being an inferior education have to pay more than those who get the superior model.

9. Future lines of development and policy options

The main challenge in applying telematics to basic education is to find ways of achieving potential benefits without widening the gap between the information-rich and information-poor. In many countries the new technologies are of limited application in primary schools where other needs take priority. In contrast, they are of major potential benefit for teacher education and for strengthening the rapidly expanding junior-secondary cycle. Broadcasting, linked with community-based activities, and distance education have a role to play in adult basic education, because of their potential reach and modest cost, whether for a formal curriculum or for non-formal purposes. National campaigns on AIDS prevention are an obvious and high priority. Distance-education methods have a record of success in supporting extension agents but have so far been under-exploited for this purpose.

Use of new communication technologies will not allow developing countries to leapfrog the industrialised world by introducing a technology-based form of basic education. Children need to learn in a school, while the need for technical infrastructure and training all limit the extent to which the technologies can replace conventional education. For most least developed countries (LDCs) the cost of computer-based education far exceeds the cost of conventional education.

Sound decisions about the use of information and communication policies will be facilitated where there is a national communications policy and a policy for educational communications within it. This will embrace linguistic and cultural issues. It will need to take account of the use to be made by the education service of the new technologies and of education's role in providing education about them. In developing such a policy a key need, as yet unmet by research, is for full and disinterested information about the costs and effects of the various technologies available for education.

10. Conclusions

Eight main conclusions follow from the evidence and analysis.

There is no alternative to primary school. Technology-based alternatives have not thrived.

Computers have been used in primary schools but in a modest way, sometimes mainly for games. They are more important higher up the education system.

Radio can enrich and extend basic education at costs much more modest than those of television or computers.

The demand for junior-secondary education and the potential of the technologies suggest that use of the latter should be expanded to raise quality and widen access at junior-secondary level.

There are promising models for out-of-school equivalence at this level.

Despite the mixed record of non-formal education, the social and educational needs of adults are so great that there is a case for continuing and expanding use of the technologies here.

National policies need to be developed that seek to use new technologies cost-effectively while avoiding widening the gap between the information-rich and the information-poor.

The use of communication technologies for teachers and extension agents, with its multiplier effect, merits investment as a cost-effective way of raising educational quality.

◆◆◆

3

Community Partnerships in Education: Dimensions, Variations, and Implications

Article 7 of the 1990 World Declaration on Education for All observed that national, regional and local educational authorities have a unique obligation to provide basic education for all. However, the Declaration continued, these bodies cannot be expected to supply every human, financial or organisational requirement for this task.

To help achieve the goal, the Declaration suggested that:

> New and revitalised partnerships at all levels will be necessary: partnerships among all sub-sectors and forms of education...partnerships between government and non-governmental organisations, the private sector, local communities, religious groups and families, (Artical 7)

This study focuses on one of those types of partnerships: between governments and communities.

The notion of government-community partnership was of course not new. Such partnerships had operated in a range of settings for many decades. As the architects of the Jomtien Declaration were aware, however, reoriented and extended partnerships were necessary. Such partnerships could contribute to the planning and implementation of basic education programmes, to increased effectiveness and to stronger feelings of community ownership.

The decade which followed showed the wisdom of the emphasis of partnerships. While the goals set in 1990 have not yet been fully achieved, much more has been achieved than would have been possible in the absence of partnerships.

However, deepening experience has also shown complexities. Models which work in one setting may not work in another; and models which operate well at one time may not operate so well subsequently. In many systems, greater emphasis on partnerships requires some decentralisation of structures, but governments are commonly ambivalent about loss of control. They also fear loss of efficiency and increase in inequalities in decentralised systems, and they may be uneasy about the diversity of practices which results from the increased number of decision-makers.

A further dimension concerns the role of the state. Operation of effective partnerships may require radical changes in this domain. Changes which require significant reduction in the role of the state may be particularly uncomfortable to government personnel and may also be disquieting to other members of society.

1. The meanings and dimensions of partnership

The notion of partnership implies shared decision-making, in which all partners play active roles. These roles are not necessarily equal: frameworks may have dominant and subordinate partners. However, the essence of partnership is that each actor has an independent voice and a way to shape the outcomes of negotiations. While in many settings the government is appropriately the dominant partner, this model is not and should not be, universal. In many contexts governments and communities play equal roles, and in some situations the communities are the dominant partners while governments are the subordinate ones.

Whatever the balance between the partners, ingredients which must be present include:

- willingness to respect the viewpoints of other partners;
- identification of common tasks; and
- collaboration in pursuit of ways to accomplish the tasks.

The 1990 Jomtien declaration emphasised the need for partnerships to be 'genuine'. This raises the question what a 'false' partnership might be. The chief answer would be a situation in which the major actor did not truly listen to the aspirations of the other actors, imposed its own agenda, and/or coerced others to agree.

Unfortunately, experience since the Jomtien conference has shown many examples of false partnerships as well as of genuine one. In particular, governments have commonly viewed communities as convenient providers of resources for education on models totally controlled by the governments. A situation in which communities are expected to provide pupils, materials, finance and other resources for schools which are totally controlled by governments cannot be called a genuine partnership. And the fact that such models in many countries have failed to provide education of appropriate quantity and quality is a strong reason why the objectives and nature of partnership need to be reviewed.

In some settings, it may be added, the imbalance is on the other side: communities are the dominant partners and give little voice to governments. These communities may be willing to take government resources, but are unwilling to listen to the governments' visions on how those resources should be used. This situation is less common; but it does exist, and needs to be brought into discussion to show that imbalances are not always the fault of governments. Genuine partnership, it must be stressed, requires *all* actors to respect viewpoints, to identify common tasks, and to collaborate in implementation.

Within this overall framework there are many variations in precisely who does what under what circumstances. Contexts and needs vary greatly in different parts of the world. Moreover, education is a multifacted endeavour, and each facet may need a slightly different balance in the roles of different actors. Thus the balance of control may not be the same, for example, in the matters of core curriculum, maintenance of buildings, teacher deployment and discipline of pupils. Again different models may be identified which have worked better in some settings than in others.

2. The nature of communities, and the mechanisms for partnership

The word 'community' can mean different things to different people in different circumstances. This fact requires care when analysing circumstances in particular settings.

For present purposes, the most important types of communities are:

- *geographic communities*, which embrace the individuals living in relatively small areas such as villages, districts or suburbs;
- *ethnic and racial groups*, especially ones which are minorities and which have self-help support structures;
- *religious groups* of various kinds;
- *communities based on shared family concerns*, including Parents' Associations which are based on adults' shared concerns for the welfare of their children; and
- *communities based on shared philanthropy* and in many cases operated by specifically-designated charitable and/or political bodies.

These communities are not always well organised in a formal sense. For example, not all geographic communities have formal bodies through which voices are heard and collective decisions reached. Indeed, in many settings it is difficult to state where the community begins and ends. Moreover, communities are rarely homogeneous. Most communities have sub-groups which do not always operate together and in harmony, and even in tightly-defined geographic areas some individuals and groups may not consider that residence in a particular location necessarily makes them part of a community.

Experience shows, however, that schools can themselves be important focal points for creating and fostering community identity. Many schools have formal committees which are responsible for representing parents in decisions concerning the planning, development and operation of the institutions. Many schools also have broader associations to bring together not only parents but also community members.

The existence of non-governmental organisations concerned with education deserves particular comment because their proliferation in many parts of the world was among the particularly striking aspects of the decade which followed the 1990 Jomtien Conference. In some settings this change was the result of government encouragement, but elsewhere governments were neutral or even discouraging. Whatever the causes of proliferation, it has brought a major change in circumstances and is among the elements requiring reassessment of approaches and strategies.

3. Conclusions

Even with the advent of globalisation, the different regions and sub-regions of the world of course remain very diverse. No single formula for partnership can be presented to take account of all types of circumstances. Appropriate policies for rural areas may be very different from those for cities; policies for dynamic communities will differ from those for passive communities; and the varied historical legacies of colonialism, politics and economics have different implications for different societies.

Nevertheless, the architects of the World Declaration on Education for All were wise to emphasise the need for partnerships and their message remains as valid at the beginning of the new century as it was in 1990. In the search for appropriate partnerships between governments and communities, much can be learned from comparative analysis. This study does not provide a single recipe for success which can be utilised everywhere. But it does show some models which have worked well in some settings and it shows some pitfalls which in other settings have caused frustration and failure.

Partnerships will remain one of the keys to the achievement of appropriate quality and quantity of education for all. Although this study focuses only on government and community partnerships, some of its lessons apply to all types of partnerships. All actors in educational processes need to review the nature of their existing collaboration and to identify ways in which partnerships can be strengthened in pursuit of the common goal.

◆◆◆

Early Childhood Care and Development

This review of early childhood care and development (ECCD)[1] has been commissioned[2] as a contribution to the EFA 2000 Assessment. ECCD emerged at Jomtien as an important extension of the more traditional approach to basic education in which education began with entrance into school. Specifically, the Framework for Action fashioned at the World Conference set as one of the targets to be considered by signatories in their plans for the 1990s: *'Expansion of early childhood care and development activities, including family and community interventions, especially for poor, disadvantaged and disabled children'*. The World Declaration on Education for All stated that *'Learning begins at birth. This calls for early childhood care and initial education. These can be provided through arrangements involving families, communities or institutional programmes, as appropriate.'*

The information base for the review and analysis comes from: (1) a literature review, (2) available country reports prepared as part of the more general EFA Assessment and (3) a survey of "knowledgeable people" involved in ECCD and coming from different geographic, disciplinary and organisational settings.

1. Changing contexts

A brief overview of differences among contexts and of the

dominant, forceful and varied changes that are occurring in the world in which ECCD is embedded suggests that we should be humble with respect to our expectations about what world conferences can accomplish. Continuing industrialisation and urbanisation, social prejudices, debt burdens, national conflicts and growing poverty and inequality combine with the extension of the HIV/AIDS pandemic, shifting policies and values linked to globalisation, economic recessions in some countries, and differential access to technology and resources create new demands, but also barriers to achieving desired ECCD goals. Therefore, modest gains should be celebrated and talk of 'advances' must be kept in context. Moreover, the variety among settings and the immense differences in the timing and incidence of particular trends for particular countries, with accompanying differences in their influence on early childhood care and development, lead us to believe that generalisations must be tempered, even when focusing on the 'Majority World'[3]. Policies and programmes must be adjusted to particular contexts.

2. Tendencies since 1990

In the well-being of children

Over the past ten years, major advances have been made worldwide in reducing infant and child mortality. Important declines have occurred also in levels of malnutrition in some countries and the consumption of micronutrients has improved. However, malnutrition continues at high levels in many countries, particularly in rural areas. Moreover, there is evidence that feeding programmes, unless combined with other measures may not be particularly effective in decreasing malnutrition.

Unfortunately, very few countries provide us with measures of the psycho-social well-being of young children or of their learning during their early years. Improvements are inferred from changes in subsequent school performance and retention, but these are at best indirect measures of a child's general development or psycho-social well-being.

In ECCD enrolments

As of this writing (January 1999), it has been possible to obtain access to sixty-four country assessments, almost all of which provide statistics on enrolments. Missing are reports from Africa and the Middle East. Nevertheless, the documentation that is available from the EFA country reviews, together with earlier documentation (reports of regional meetings, UNICEF annual reports, special studies, etc.) suggests the following:

- A general tendency has been for enrolments to increase since 1990. In some cases enrolment has decreased, particularly (and massively) in countries that were part of the Soviet Union (until 1991) and in countries of Eastern Europe that were previously under Soviet influence.
- Although there are some cases of large, and even rather dramatic, growth during the period, the increases can more generally be characterised as small and marginal.
- The variation among countries in levels of access is huge, ranging from almost zero to virtually 100 per cent, with a general tendency for enrolment to be related to GNP.
- Attention continues to be concentrated on 'preschooling' and on children aged 4 to 6, particularly on the year just prior to primary school. A corollary is that few children under 4 in the Majority World are being attended in organised ECCD programmes.
- Urban children are more likely to be enrolled in some sort of ECCD programme than rural children.

- Children from families that are better off are more likely to be enrolled than children from families with few resources.
- For most countries for whom reports were received there is relative gender parity in enrolments. There are, however, a few exceptions where boys are favoured, particularly in countries of the Middle East.
- The relative roles of the State, the private and social sectors, and communities in providing ECCD services varies widely among countries; whereas the trend is towards greater government involvement in some, a tendency for growth of the private sector dominates in others.

As suggested above, these generalisations need to be tempered and a more detailed analysis is needed based on the country reviews which, at best will provide a cloudy picture given the current state of information collection systems.

3. In Conditions Affecting ECCD Programming

Knowledgeable people and country reports have identified a wide range of advances in conditions, differing from country to country, that affect the delivery of ECCD services and their potential effect on the well-being of children. These include:

1. Conceptual shifts and changes in the knowledge base and its dissemination.

The most frequently mentioned (by survey respondents) advance in knowledge related to ECCD during the 1990s was an advancc in our understanding of how the brain develops and functions. Also mentioned with some frequency was a growing body of knowledge coming from research studies and programme evaluations showing long-term benefits of early intervention programmes for children at risk. Other new avenues of research that are beginning to influence practice include studies of 'resilience', conditions under which programmes can have a negative affect on child development, and childrearing practices and patterns.

Conceptual shifts that seem to be 'in process' include movement towards: 1) placing greater emphasis on social and cultural influences on the process of development, replacing a behaviourist viewpoint and complementing a more individual and 'constructivist' view of development and giving renewed importance to the role of the teacher and to the place of language in the teaching/learning process; and 2) questioning the concept of universal 'best practices' grounded in developmental psychology, accompanied by greater attention to discovering, respecting, and incorporating cultural differences into thinking about how early childhood education and care 'should' occur, with viewpoints grounded in anthropology, sociology and ethics.

Also noted were conceptual shifts in the manner in which planning, programming and implementing organisations are thinking about their task of moving knowledge into action, involving, for instance:1) viewing early childhood programming within a broader framework of poverty alleviation or transitions to democracy, 2) linking the concept of «holistic» development to integral programming cutting across sectoral lines; 3) preventing—as constrasted with 'compensating'—problems once they occur. 4) In the air also is a change in how governments se their role, with a tendency to shift at least some of the burden of providing services from exclusive government responsibility to partnerships and sometimes to the market-place through 'privatisation.' 5) The Convention on the Rights of the Child, and perhaps to a lesser extent the conceptual frame provided at Jomtien, are helping to shift thinking, from a «needs» perspective which tends to be associated more directly with focused or 'targeted' interventions to a universal 'rights' perspective, and from early attention as 'pre-schooling' to an ECCD perspective.

The knowledge base has also been fed by experience in the form of many programmes and projects mounted during the 1990s and earlier that are deemed 'effective' and that provide a wealth of ideas and options.

Although the above may sound encouraging, these shifts in knowledge and concept are slow and there is a lament by many that new knowledge does not seem to transfer into changes in policies or programming. In part that is related to a feeling that the dissemination process is deficient, despite noted increases in publications, forums, inter-country discussions, web-sites and the emergence of regional and national as well as international networks.

2. Change in attitudes/awareness.

Related to the growth of a knowledge base and to its dissemination is an increased awareness, within governments and the non-governmental organisation community, and among policy-makers and intellectuals, regarding: 1) the importance of early childhood care and education (and particularly of the earliest years), 2) what early childhood development is (for instance, recognition that it is an active, holistic and integral process involving the child as a person) and 3) how to go about fostering it. In the third category is included a new openness to:

- diversifying attention, broadening the range of options and including programmes directed to family and community as well as to the child;
- acceptance of non-formal approaches (but not as 'second best');
- developing home-school partnerships;
- working with non-governmental organisations;
- inter-sectoral collaboration and co-ordination; and
- thinking beyond enrolment to quality.

Although examples may be cited for all of the above, it is clear that greater awareness often does not translate into changes in policy or programmes; indeed, these same topics are included in the category of problems to be overcome and in recommendations of lines of action that need to be pursued.

3. Changes in policies and in legal and legislative frameworks for programming internationally and nationally.

Country reports and survey respondents often noted specific changes in laws, the development of policies and the explicit inclusion of ECCD in national plans as advances in the field of ECCD. At the same time, the lack of good and comprehensive laws and policies, particularly for children under 3, characterises too many countries. And, there is considerable criticism of some of the broader government policies (for instance, economic adjustment policies) that affect ECCD indirectly and are often linked to international agency policies.

4. The availability of resources.

There is no doubt that the overall level of international financing available for ECCD has increased a great deal since 1990. At the same time, questions have been raised about the style of funding organisations and about the national capacity to use available international funds well. The picture is not so clear with respect to national budgets where some important increases and some decreases have occurred over the decade. Although it has not been possible to determine from country reports the level of funding available for ECCD (with a very few exceptions), the scant evidence suggests that government funding is very low (often less than 2 per cent of the total education budget). In most of Africa, the Middle East, the Caribbean and parts of Asia, major responsibility for ECCD is left to families, communities and non-governmental organisations. And, while few of the people surveyed point immediately to lack of funding as a barrier to advance in the ECCD field, there is a pronounced feeling that the filed is under-funded, that public financial support is low and unstable, and that the lack of resources is an important problem.

A similar picture appears for human resources, with indications of advances in professional formation in many countries set against a strong feeling that human resources are lacking and that training is needed at all levels, but particularly at local levels as decentralisation occurs.

5. Organisational bases, strengthened and consolidated, both governmental and non-governmental.

Observations by survey respondents in this category are varied indeed, but many are related to on-going processes of diversification and decentralisation, covering such changes as: new strength in local non-governmental organisations and municipal governments, the incorporation of early childhood development into different sectoral programmes. Mention is made of the formation of inter-sectoral committees and councils.

As with other categories, this set of advances is cited for a limited number of settings and must be set against others in which the organisational weakness of non-governmental organisations, and local organisations and governmental bodiesis emphasised and the failure to co-ordinate actions is pointed out.

4. Changes in ECCD practice

Some shifts have occurred in the processes of training and teaching, which, together with creation of new curricula and better materials, are intended to redefine and improve programme quality. However, these advances are modest. More attention has been given to increasing enrolments than to improving quality. For instance, although there have been important advances in the number and quality of ECCD training programmes at various levels, training continues to be seen by many as the most important need in the ECCD field. And, whereas it is possible to cite curriculum changes in some countries, moving the field toward active learning, play and guided discovery, the tendency to treat early education as an extension downward of primary school continues and cultural constructions of curricula involving indigenous communities are rare. The good intentions fostered through training, and curricula and materials are often undercut by an outrageously large ratio of children to adults in ECCD centres, a tendency to treat adults in ECCD parental education programmes as children and an inability to incorporate a community dimension into larger-scale ECCD programmes.

5. Problems and Proposals: Where do we go from here?

This section sets out problem areas and needs as identified by survey respondents and as found in recent publications. The following listing, which is expressed in term of 'deficits', should not be interpreted to mean that countries have not made advances. Indeed, in addressing these deficits, it would be well to begin by securing and extending the gains already made in these areas.

1. Weak political will.

The need continues to convince politicians, policy-makers, programmers, and education officials, often now at local levels, of the importance of ECCD. To create will, we need to develop:

- better strategies of communicating, lobbying and advocating; and
- a better information base, with improved indicators, statistics, monitoring systems, studies and evaluations.

2. Weak policy and legal frameworks.

To formulate and strengthen policy we need to:

- undertake analytical studies of existing policies affecting children, looking beyond narrowly conceived educational policies to, for instance social welfare, health, and labour policies that affect child care and development during the early years:
- seek conformity with the Convention on the Rights of the Child, incorporating principles of the best interests of the child, non-discrimination and participation.
- work closely with the legal profession; and
- establish norms and standards (for private as well as public, and including provisions for constant (revision) that are not so rigid or high as to be unworkable but that will assure positive attention to children.

3. Lack of, or poor use of, financial resources.

ECCD programmes generally command a small portion of governmental budgets, relative to percentage of young children in the population. In budgetary terms, children (and especially young children) are clearly not placed first. There is, therefore, a need to:

- increase allocations to ECCD in national budgets and make more permanent commitments to such funding;
- strengthen the capacity of states and municipalities to obtain resources for ECCD;
- seek cost-effective approaches, including quality community-based non-formal approaches to ECCD;
- explore more vigorously such alternative (to government budgets) avenues of funding as debt swaps, philanthropic contributions, and private sector involvement;

- co-ordinate the increase of financial resources with attention to the capacity to handle such resources and the strengthening of human resources; and
- provide access to central pots of money by local organisation so as to respond better to local demand expressed in proposals originating in communities.

4. Uniformity (lack of options).

The bureaucratically convenient tendency to extend the same programme to all children conflicts with the need to tailor ECCD programmes to cultural, geographic, economic and age differences. This tendency is reinforced by the notion that ECCD is the same as 'pre-school' which, in turn, is simply an extension downward of primary schooling. We need, therefore, to:

- think in terms of complementary and varied approaches to ECCD that include family and community-based programmes;
- involve non-governmental organisations more actively as partners;
- decentralise programme responsibility as well as administrative responsibility, with attention to building local capacity; and
- construct culturally relevant programmes with local communities rather than impose ECCD practices from the centre.

5. Poor quality.

There is a pressing need to:

- re-examine training and supervision and to provide sound training (both pre-service and in-service) at all levels in with respect to a diversity of ECCD approaches;
- reduce the number of children (or families) per education/ care agent;

- improve and reformulate curricula, taking into account not only 'best practices' but also local definition of what constitutes 'best practices';
- draw upon existing experience in a more systematic way; and
- establish better systems to monitor and evaluate both children and programmes.

6. Lack of attention to particular populations.

The following 'disadvantaged' populations need to be given greater attention: low-income, rural, indigenous, girls, HIV/AIDS, children 0-3, pregnant and lactating mothers, working mothers, fathers.

7. Lack of co-ordination.

If a holistic and integrated notion of learning and development is to be honoured and if resources are to be used more effectively, greater co-ordination is needed firstly, among government programmes of health, welfare, social security, nutrition, education, rural or community development, etc., secondly, within the education sector, especially between ECCD and primary schooling and finally, between governmental and non-governmental organisations. We need to.

- create inter-sectoral, inter-organisational co-ordinating bodies;
- construct joint programmes crossing bureaucratic boundaries;
- strengthen the ability of families and communities to call upon and bring together services that are at present offered in an unco-ordinated fashion;
- seek agreement on the populations that are most in need of attention and direct services to those populations in a converging manner; and

- build partnerships (a clearer definition is needed of the roles of the state and civil society and of forms of partnership).

8. Narrow conceptualisation.

The conceptual frameworks guiding programmes intended to improve early childhood care and development and early learning have come primarily from developmental psychology and from formal education. There is a need to go beyond the knowledge that these fields can provide to incorporate broader views with cultural, social and ethical dimensions brought to bear. There is a need also to relate ECCD programming, conceptually and operationally, to other programme lines that begin from analyses of children's rights, poverty, working mothers, rural development, special needs, street children, refugees, adolescents, gender, etc.

6. Where should the emphasis be placed? Where should we concentrate efforts?

The first answer to this question must be 'it depends'. Regions and countries (and parts of countries) bring to the table extremely different conditions and cultural views, and are at very different points in a process. It is therefore inappropriate to try and set general priorities for action in all situations. In some places emphasis must be given to advocacy and to getting the policy and legal frameworks right. In others, emphasis needs to be given to problems related to combating HIV/AIDS. In others, facilities need to be repaired.

Consistent with this posture, the second answer to the question must be 'Each country (or perhaps even municipality) must take stock and decide upon its priorities.'

Having said the above, it does seem appropriate to present my own biased opinion of areas that seem to need special emphasis and that seem to stretch across many settings and to suggest some general guidelines that represent the author's particular view of what needs to be put front and centre as the field evolves.

1. Some possible areas of special interest.

A. Training and supervision. Starting from the premise that the quality of programmes will be only as good as the people who operate them, it is logical to place emphasis on assuring that ECCD people at various levels are well motivated and are part of a continuous process of training.

B. Supporting, educating and involving parents and other family members. Parents and other family members will continue to be the main influences on young children's lives for the foreseeable future, especially for children under 3 or 4 years of age. Perhaps the greatest and most lasting effects on a child's learning and development can come from improvements in the capacity of parents to provide a supportive environment for learning and development. As suggested earlier, there are many possible way to support and work with parents and family members and the particular combination of how to go about this work will vary with conditions.

C. Evaluation and monitoring. Giving priority to building monitoring and evaluation systems derives from more than an academic bias. Among the lessons learned from successful programmes is that effectiveness is fostered if programmes develop slowly and are monitored and adjusted regularly. The information that comes from monitoring and evaluation will serve advocacy purposes as well as policy and administrative purposes. The information should help the process of reconceptualisation that many survey respondents felt is necessary. The failure of EFA process to provide for adequate indicators for the ECCD area testifies to the need for work in this area.

2. Possible guidelines: a starting point for discussion

- Take a holistic view of the child and of the learning and development process, adopting cross-sectoral policies.
- Concentrate on the well-being of children and not on the size of particular programmes or on building bureaucracies.
- Begin with pre-natal attention.
- Include the excluded. Focus on equity.
- Be family-focused and community-based, fostering participation.
- Seek cultural relevance, determined by those involved, and accommodation, beginning where people are, building on inherent strengths.
- Build child-focused partnerships.
- Seek cost-effectiveness, broadly defined.
- Avoid formulas. Be open to diversity and to complementary approaches.
- Seek quality.
- Incorporate monitoring and evaluation into programmes from the outset.

7. In closing

In this international forum, organised by international organisations, it seems appropriate to reflect on the role that has been, and can be, played by international organisations in promoting and supporting programmes directed at improving the care and development of young children. In gathering information for this review of ECCD, it was clear that international organisations have been given credit for and have played several important roles in helping ECCD to extend and improve. These include assistance in providing frameworks for analysis and action (Jomtien, the Convention), strengthening the knowledge base and disseminating information (supporting research, evaluation, monitoring, the creation of networks, publications, etc.), advocating (by organising international forums, by negotiating conditions for financial support and by marshalling the media), as well as by providing technical and financial support. These efforts have certainly contributed to many of the 'advances' noted earlier. At the same time, it is important to recognise that these forms of assistance represent interventions that imply certain value positions, that they depend for their result as much on the manner in which the assistance is offered as they do on the amount of assistance provided, and that can have negative as well as positive consequences. Consider the following:

1. Frameworks and knowledge—the basis for lobbying and constructing ECCD programmes—continue to originate, for the most part, in the Minority World. Accordingly a tension often arises between 'received truth' linked to the Minority World knowledge base and values guiding an agency, and local knowledge linked to another set of values rooted in some part of the Majority World. These may overlap, but are different. Within the international community there are tensions as well. For instance, the universal rights framework being espoused by some can conflict with a needs-based approach and 'targeting'. The way in which these tensions are handled determines to some degree how 'success' is defined for projects and can wind up creating a barrier to action because agreement is lacking implications:

- Although the current attention to involving all "stakeholders" in the process of creating a project represents an important step toward breaking with the past tendency to impose, we are far from making that participation real and meaningful. Additional work is needed to change past styles and methods.

- Major changes are needed in the consultant system which continues to depend for technical assistance on Minority World consultants (myself included). More efforts should be put into drawing upon local knowledge and experience, embodied in local consultants.

2. Because programming for ECCD is at an early stage in many countries, it is possible to construct programmes in innovative ways, taking into account differing conditions, seeking convergence, and involving local communities in the process. This implies a need to move slowly, to experiment and reinvent, to build collaborative enterprises, to nurture, to support a variety of initiatives and to build capacity. Unfortunately, these needs run counter to social and political desires to move quickly so that as many people as possible are served. They run counter to bureaucratic desires to simplify administration by providing the same service to all and to avoid collaboration across sectoral lines. And they run counter to the characteristics of many international organisations where promotion and success is equated with the numbers of children and families served, with the ability to promote the particular doctrine of the agency, and/or with the ability to move money. The quantitative focus and a sense of urgency inhibits developing quality programmes, current rhetoric notwithstanding. Implications:

- Place less emphasis on expanding enrolments and on extending one particular programme to all; place more emphasis on equality, beginning with solid support for training, with local input into what is considered a quality programme, and with a vision of 'scale' as the sum of many efforts.

- Take a longer-term view and being slowly; avoid overloading systems financially with too much money too soon. Be sure cash is accompanied by capacity-building.

- Develop loan and grant instruments that are demand driven rather than supply-driven, that allow varied responses to differentiated local demands.
- Find ways to work more meaningfully on the ground with non-governmental organisations.

For many international organisations, the changes suggested above constitute huge challenge that goes to the heart of how organisations function. In a meeting where commitment to change by national governments is being sought, a parallel commitment might be asked of international organisations that goes well beyond a resource commitment and includes re-examination of values and the ethics of intervention styles and modes of operation.

Notes :

1. Early Childhood Care and Development (ECCD) is used throughout the document, taken from the Jomtien Framework for Action. 'Learning' and 'education' are embedded in development. The phrase is purposely chosen to connote a broad and integral view of learning and education. Other valid terms we might have used include: Early Childhood Care and (Initial) Education (taken from the Jomtien Declaration). Early Childhood Education and Care (OECD), Early Childhood Care for Survival, Growth and Development (UNICEF) or Early Childhood Development (World Bank).
2. By UNICEF on behalf of the EFA Forum.
3. In this document we will use the concept of Majority World in preference to phrases such as 'developing countries' or 'Third World' or 'The South'.

◆◆◆

5

Education for All and Children who are Excluded

Each One Counts. The Convention on the Rights of the Child affirms the right of *all* children to relevant and good quality education. It confirms and extends the belief of many cultures that there is a social contract and moral commitment of the part of States to ensure the equity and well-being of all citizens. It brings the moral weight of an international instrument to propel a major shift in perspective for States and donors as they implement action to achieve Education For All (EFA).

The Convention on the Rights of the Child reconfirms the EFA imperative of an 'expanded vision' of education: that all children have the right to learn at all stages of their development, and to do so in ways which are appropriate and easily accessible. It reconfirms that this learning must be such that it contributes to children's physical, psychosocial, emotional and intellectual development. It should enhance their capacity to earn a living, participate in the decisions of their society and live in peace and dignity. Increases in the percentage of children reached are important, but are no longer sufficient. Quality counts. All children have the right of access to *effective* opportunities for learning. Exceptions cannot simply be argued away on the basis of 'especially difficult circumstances'.

The *exclusion of children constitutes a broadly based and intricate web of human rights violations.* The exclusion of children is in itself a broad-brush phenomenon. Millions of children are made vulnerable by living in circumstances of poverty, socio-cultural marginalisation, geographic isolation, racial and/or gender bias. They are further encumbered with corollary burdens of disease and disability, sexual exploitation, indentured and injurious labour, or forced involvement in civil and military conflict. The exclusion of these children from education is simply one more manifestation of this web of rights violations. But it is a particularly tragic one. Without access to good quality education, children are denied the opportunity to acquire the knowledge, capacities and self-confidence necessary, as children and later as adults, to act on their own, behalf in changing the circumstances that are excluding them.

Exclusion is interactive and comprehensive. It touches all aspects of the lives of affected children, resulting either in their having no access to education or in their being poorly served when they are enrolled. In consequence, they repeat, drop out or graduate without actually learning. Being excluded from education is not a single event in a child's life; nor is it a single process. Rather, exclusion from education involves a pattern of personal, socio-cultural, economic and institutional factors which together act to keep a child from participating in effective and organised learning experiences.

Three broad types of dimensions or factors are involved in this syndrome of exclusion; it is in the specific characteristics and interactions of each of these where the causes, consequences, the scope, severity and dynamics of exclusion in any one setting will be found:

i) *contextual*: Environmental and demographic pressures, institutional structures and technological infrastructure, and especially political and economic systems;

ii) *socio-cultural*: belief and value systems, indigenous knowledge and skills, family structures, community arrangements; and

iii) *relational*: decision-making systems and communication, resource allocation patterns, negotiation and conflict resolution mechanisms, gender and age relations.

Further, exclusion happens at every level of society: children, their families and communities; schools and education systems; national education policy communities; and the society as a whole. International agencies are also influential in each of these, of course, Specifically:

- Children within the family and the community.
- The school within the education system.
- National education policy within the society and international community.

1. Exclusion at the micro level: The school

Schools exclude at the micro level when they are not learner-friendly, do not support their teachers as professionals and do not welcome families as partners.

- Schools exclude when they fail to create a culture of peace, when they fail to take affirmative and uncompromising action to end all forms of harassment, abuse and violence.
- Schools exclude when they do not reach out proactively to the families of children who are most vulnerable.
- Schools exclude these children by not taking their families into account, by not creating programmes expressly to link them into the educational processes their children are experiencing.
- Schools exclude when they fail to concern themselves with those children who do not turn up.
- Schools contribute to exclusion by not putting systems in place for formally noticing and tracking the non-attendee or truant.
- Exclusion happens to both individuals alone and to individuals as members of groups or categories of children.

- Schools exclude by costing too much, directly and by implication.
- Schools exclude by not being sufficiently accountable—to their teachers, students or parents.

2. Exclusion at the meso level: The education bureaucracy

- The education bureaucracy excludes at the meso level by failing to recognise the diversity of learners within its purview.
- The education bureaucracy excludes children when it fails to provide their teachers with the learning and professional status they need to be effectively competent, responsible and motivated.
- Education systems exclude when they fail to provide teachers regular in-service professional development and moral support from qualified and learning-oriented supervisors.
- By failing to provide teachers on-going professional support, education systems most seriously exclude through a message that says 'conscientious teaching is the least prominent and most thankless of the activities they (teachers) are expected to perform.'
- Education bureaucracies exclude by being 'predicated on the achievement of the "successful", rather than on an inclusive education[1] which aims to improve the problem-solving and critical learning skills of all pupils and not just a select few.'
- Children already at risk are made more vulnerable to exclusion when the system's testing procedures fail to reflect their individual learning characteristics and home backgrounds and to accommodate teaching to these.
- The education bureaucracy excludes children when it persists in creating inappropriate and irrelevant curriculum and materials of poor pedagogical quality.

3. Exclusion at the macro level: National education policy

- Government and education policies exclude at the macro level in two broad ways. By commission, they actively deny children's right to education through the regulations they apply—restrictive enrolment criteria, for example, or policies that *segregate children with disabilities into institutional arrangements without professionally competent staff, effective co-ordination with the mainstream education system or support to parents.* They also exclude by omission, failing to make "education for all" a broad societal philosophy and articulated priority; or failing to implement any pro-child policies which do exist in serious, systematic ways.
- National government and education policy-making bodies exclude by not seriously or comprehensively identifying barriers to education for families and children at risk, or creating opportunities to enable their participation.
- National systems exclude when they purposively segregate children with special learning needs.
- Macro levels exclude by failing systematically to assess variations in learning achievement across the country.
- Education policy-making excludes when it segregates the formal "legitimate" school system from the less worthy "rest".
- Macro policies exclude by insisting on centralised and inflexible control over standards, approaches and methods, which are not relevant to vulnerable communities.

How education systems exclude children potentially concerns all children, to some degree. The concern of this paper, and critical for the focus of global action in support of education during the next fifteen years, however, are those children who are affected in a major way by these exclusionary forces. They are the children, chiefly (but not solely) in developing countries, living in conditions of extreme poverty and social marginalisation. They are children who, whether on their own or through their families, are unlikely to be able to break the exclusionary downward cycle. They are, therefore, the children for whom national systems and the international community must take significant affirmative and persistent action both to change the basic conditions of poverty and exclusion in their lives overall, and to design and implement inclusive, effective education.

More specifically, they are children who

- are not considered to "fit" into majority-based classrooms: ethnic minority and scheduled caste children; children of different cultures, speaking other than a national language; or whose dysfunctional or broken family or life on the street lead them to be stereotyped as children incapable or unworthy of learning and appropriately kept out of school.
- contradict locally accepted norms of who can or should learn: girls in general and pregnant girls in particular; children with disabilities or affected by HIV/AIDS.
- cannot afford the cost or the time of schooling: children from chronically poor urban and rural families or for whom economic crises have created newly-jobless families; working and street children; children who are the fall-out of SAPs.
- are not free or available to participate: geographically isolated children in coastal fishing communities or remote mountain areas; child soldiers; unregistered migrants; children of transients, seasonal workers and nomadic communities.
- are living in the context of disaster: children in war, refugee children and children displaced by destruction of their physical environment.

What does exclusion look like? Somewhat arbitrarily, these have been grouped according to who the children are, where they are (i.e. the circumstances in which they find themselves), and what they are doing. These categories are not mutually exclusive. The excluded child is, for example, a *girl* who is *working* as a flower seller *on the street* of an impoverished Brazilian slum; he is an *adolescent boy* from a *hilltribe community* forced to *serve in one of the drug militias* of the Golden Triangle. The differentiation into the who, where and what of exclusion is intended to provide perspective, to make the concept more accessible and actionable in terms of thinking about specific focus constraints and entry points.

"Who" these children are, then concerns those characteristics that are effectively "given", the essence of the child: gender, ethnicity and race; age (for that period); basic intellectual and physical capacities; background experience and personal history. These are the bases on which the child must be accepted as a learner, and around which the society, the education system and the school must organise to ensure a relevant and effective learning experience. They are characteristics that cannot be used as justification for exclusion.

"Where" concerns the context in which the child lives, or has been placed. It concerns the surrounding conditions which exclude children by failing to allow for their (and their families') basic rights and needs, including access to good education. It shifts the focus from the child to those responsible for ensuring the protection and development of this and all children, pursuant to the commitments of the Convention on the Rights of the Child. It forces consideration not of how the child must change to fit into school, but of how the barriers presented by the school and the wider socio-economic, cultural and political environment can be removed, or their negative impacts mitigated, so as to ensure the child's does "fit".

"What they are doing" concerns both the who and where of exclusion. It concerns how children, based on the individual and social resources and personal interests they bring, are managing or coping with the conditions of their lives. This includes consideration of how ready the child is to engage in learning and/or to participate in education, given the other activities and concerns he or she faces. The focus here is on collaboration. It concerns how those responsible for children's well-being can most effectively know, and co-operate with, those children to design and implement action appropriate to ensuring their effective and relevant education (as well as health care, social services, justice, etc.). A perspective on what excluded children are doing forces situation analyses and interventions to be more refined and tailored; to consider, for example, what working children are working at and where, with what risk and how much "space" they have for learning. It forces interventions to consider specially what a child is doing on the street, in a conflict zone or in an isolated rural school. It forces consideration of how education can be made to suit children as they are now, and to help them move forward.

Globally, under all categories, the answer to this is that, **most, frequently, the excluded children are girls.** Gender continues to be the major causal factor in children being left out, and pushed out, of school. The denial of a girl's right to education remains a pernicious and persistent characteristic of many societies on a purposive basis, by reason of culture and family choice-making.

The basic *question* of education is simple enough: "why is it that schools throughout the world fail to teach so many children successfully?" Beyond saying that societies are not trying hard enough, the *answer* is not so simple. Exclusion is a layered phenomenon. Underlying conditions keep children out: poverty, discrimination, and communal violence. Systemic factors push them out: unsafe and insecure schools, unqualified or unmotivated teachers, inflexible schedules and irrelevant curriculum. Individual and family situations hold them back; values or other priorities push formal education aside.

While there has been progress since Jomtien in extending the quality and scope of education to many children, progress for excluded children would seem only marginal. The questions at least are clearer, and by extending the decade the world has given itself more time to try to answer them. Some of the more persistent threads of debate include:

- focusing directly on excluded children and/or more broadly on the disabling causal conditions;
- creating high quality and accessible formal school systems and/or broadening the framework to recognise early childhood and non-formal programmes as integral parts of an expanded vision;
- intervening through national-level advocacy and/or through direct context-specific action with families and communities; and
- working within closely-controlled, well-resourced pilot programmes and/or venturing directly onto the level of open-ended, real-life "scale".

In extending the EFA deadline another fifteen years, Amman gave the world more time. It also acknowledged the world's failure to respect the right of all children to an education. In effect, the new deadline of 2015 legitimises the loss of another generation. In addition to debates, then, there are challenges:

- Deal seriously with poverty.
- Make the affected children visible
- Generate better analyses of what is happening in the field.
- Make these analyses participatory.
- Make the framework wide enough.
- Focused action is necessarily co-ordinated action.
- Engage in serious and sustained introspection.

Note

1. The term "inclusive" is used throughout this text to define a philosophy of/approach to education, and to a quality of school, which are in active, purposive opposition to exclusion. In this, "inclusive education" is meant in its popular sense, but reinforced by the international commitment made in the Salamanca World Conference to education which "recognises diversity and caters for *all* learners" irrespective of the particular intellectual, physical, emotional, socio-cultural or experiential "conditions they bring with them to the learning process.

◆◆◆

Education in Crisis: The Impact and Lessons of the East Asian Financial Shock 1997-99

With the long-term benefits of education in mind, this review asks how the East Asian financial crisis affected education, measured by indicators such as enrolment, drop-out and continuation rates. It also examines how local authorities, non-government organisations, bilateral donors and international agencies helped mitigate the detrimental effects of the crisis. The study focuses on two countries, Indonesia and Thailand, while less thoroughly exploring three others, the Republic of Korea, the Philippines and Malaysia. There are two reasons—one organisational and one practical—for this selectivity. First, it allows for an in-depth analysis of the two countries. Second, there are, so far, few surveys on the impact of the crisis it the Republic of Korea, the Philippines and Malaysia. In closing, the paper tries to draw up some lessons for responses to future crises.

1. The importance of education

Both theory and empirical evidence suggest that education—in particular, primary and lower secondary education—is vital to economic growth. 'New' neoclassical theories hold that growth is driven by technological change, which is perceived as an endogenous, separate factor in the production process. It follows that education promotes economic growth through increased individual productivity spurred by the acquisition of new skills and attitudes as well as through accumulation of knowledge itself. Many empirical surveys, such as the World Bank's *East Asian Miracle* (1993), indicate that investments in education yield high returns in low—and middle—income countries. Financial shocks may, however, upset the growth-encouraging physical capital-human capital balance. When export prices plummet, the stock market crashes, the currency collapses, or bonds default, people—the market as well as the government—may lose their long-term perspective. Both households and authorities look to cut their spending on items that do not reap an immediate benefit, education being in a vulnerable position. One key finding of studies that have explored the impact of financial-economic shocks on education is that the lowest income groups tend to suffer the most.

2. The East Asian Crisis

Between 1990 and 1996, the five countries reviewed here—with the exception of the Philippines— enjoyed annual gross domestic product (GDP) growth rates of between 7 and 9 per cent. The boom ended when the Thai Baht's fall sent the East Asian economies into a vicious circle where intensifying panic rapidly caused a break-down of the financial markets. As a result, the five countries experienced dramatic drops in economic growth. The social impacts of these economic effects are transmitted through several channels: increased under-and unemployment, reduced labour-market income, increased prices and lowered net government transfers. The crisis had a moderate impact on inflation, with the important exception of Indonesia. The effect on employment was more sever, especially in Thailand and the Republic of Korea.

Indonesia

Economic and social impact: The beginning of the Indonesian part of the region-wide crisis can be marked from

21 July, 1997, when the Rupiah fell by 6 per cent against the United States dollar. As the financial shock grew into an economic and social crisis, GDP contracted by 13.8 per cent in 1998. Inflation was rampant, reaching 77 per cent in December 1998. The rise in unemployment was relatively moderate. Hardest hit, urban households experienced a 30 per cent income loss between August 1997 and August 1998.

Pre-crisis education challenges: Prior to the crisis, the key issue facing the Indonesian education system was the declining rates of primary school completion and continuation to junior secondary schools. Underlying the declining rates were increasing inefficiencies and declining school quality.

Effect on education: Survey results on enrolment vary from a slight increase to a fall of 11 per cent, depending on the age group. Secondary schools generally recorded more severe enrollment (and dropout) changes than primary schools. The lowest income groups and students living in urban areas experienced the sharpest drops in enrolments.

Key responses: Schools cut their fees. Mainly because of fierce inflation, government did not manage to maintain real education spending. On a positive note, preliminary results on the comprehensive Back-to-School campaign, which includes a scholarship programme, are encouraging.

Thailand

Economic and social impact: The Thai government was forced to float the Baht on 2 July, 1997 after a series of costly but ineffective attempts to save the increasingly overvalued currency. International Monetary Fund-led austerity measures reduced the external deficit but contributed to the recession. GDP shrank by 8 per cent in 1998. Unemployment more than doubled between February 1997 and February 1988, from 2 to 4.8 per cent. The price increases were moderate; inflation averaged 8.6 per cent in 1998. Poor, rural households suffered the biggest income losses (on average 18 per cent in real terms).

Pre-crisis education challenges: The most recent five-year education plan (the eighth since 1960) has moved away from access and equity considerations to a fresh emphasis on quality improvements in student scores and on curricula that reflect the needs of communities and the workforce. The other clear accent is on system wide reform—from teacher training to policy determination.

Effect on education: The crisis had a moderate impact on overall enrolment. Primary enrolments remained unchanged, which pre-crisis secondary enrolment increases stagnated. World Bank analyses indicate that an increasing number of students left school at important transition points. Drop-out data are somewhat ambiguous.

Key responses: Households increased their real spending on education. The government kept real education expenditure at constant levels throughout the crisis. Scholarship and loan programmes were expanded.

3. Impact on education and responses in the Republic of Korea, the Philippines and Malaysia

The Republic of Korea: Overall gross enrolment rates increased slightly between 1997 and 1998, but at the same time drop-out rates in elementary schools increased sharply. Transition rates (elementary-middle-high school) remained constant at 100 per cent. There was a shift from private to public education. House-holds largely protected education from overall expenditure cuts, but spending on private tutoring decreased sharply (by 39 per cent for the lowest income group). The government implemented a range of social protection measures.

The Philippines: Pre-crisis primary enrolment increases of roughly 3 per cent slowed to 0.7 per cent between 1997 and 1998. Secondary school enrolment decreased by 8 per cent, between 1997 and 1998. Private schools at all levels suffered the most severe losses. The drop-out ratio was negatively affected only for public secondary school students. Education's share of the total household budget increased slightly between 1997 and 1998. The government has provided, on a limited scale, scholarships and feeding programmes.

Malaysia: The crisis had a mild impact on primary and secondary education. The number of students enrolled in secondary school increased by 14 per cent between 1996 and 1998. But tertiary institutions are struggling to keep up with demand from students forced to return from universities overseas. The government managed to maintain, and even increase, its education budget during the crisis. Authorities are encouraging the funding of private institutions to increase the number of higher education spaces.

4. Synthesis

Accounting for some cautionary points—the mixed impact of, and responses to, the crisis; the varied levels of the education systems; the relative limited scope of the data gathered so far—we can draw the following general conclusions from the reviews of the five countries, particularly of Indonesia and Thailand:

- **Enrolment rates have not declined as much as feared.** Secondary enrolments seem to have been more affected than primary ones;
- **The mitigation of these enrolment declines seem to have been achieved in part through household and school-level adjustment;**
- **But also the governments' continued commitment to education,** resulting in relatively stable education expenditures—with the important exception of Indonesia—also contributed to keeping up access levels;
- **Children from poor households have been affected more severely than children from non-poor households.** One indicator is drop-outs, which shows that poor families have withdrawn their children at a greater rate than have their wealthier counterparts;

- **Some students have shifted from private to public schools, suggesting that wealthier households have felt the impact of the crisis as well; and,**
- **The economic crisis has exacerbated existing difficulties in the education systems.** A reoccurring problem in many countries is low transition rates; many primary students do not make it to junior secondary schools.

Some questions remain unanswered. Most important, the surveys reviewed reveal little about the direct impact on the *quality* of education. One can infer that quality deteriorates as resources available diminish, but there is need to measure this perceived effect more carefully.

5. Lessons for the future

Despite its limitations, this review, coupled with previous experiences with education in crisis, provides a guide for current action and a useful basis for understanding the dynamics of impact of the crisis on education.

- One long-term strategy is to **promote the proven economic and social benefits of education.** In East Asia, the shared grass-root commitment to education translated into an commendable dedication by schools, communities and families to protect schooling as the crisis broke;
- Another crisis-mitigating policy is to **make the education system as efficient as possible.** The key is flexibility—in the case of the financial-economic shock, the system should be able to cost-effectively adjust to changing conditions. Increasing private ownership may be one way to ease the burden of governments during crises.
- When economic calamity strikes, **protecting the education budgets stands out as a key concern.**

Authorities should strive to avoid reductions and delays in salaries to teachers. When reduced budgets are unavoidable, arbitrarily cutting across and board is rarely the best solution. Rather, administrators should prioritize essential items;

- **Identifying the hardest-hit groups and target assistance at these** is equally important. The ferocity of the East Asian crisis demonstrates the urgency with which crisis-mitigating policies and programmes need to be implemented. Governments must carefully track the effects of their adjustment and austerity programmes; monitoring systems should be strengthened. At the same time, authorities should not lose track of the longer-term priorities of the educational system; and,
- As a final point, there is an obvious remedy: **avoiding sickness altogether.** Within a wider perspective, the East Asian financial shock has spotlighted the need for effective early warning systems that allow authorities to pre-empt future crises. Today, in the wake of the most recent crisis, donors and governments alike are increasingly stressing the importance of transparency and good governance.

◆◆◆

Education in Situations of Emergency and Crisis

The 1990 World Conference on Education for All (EFA) set challenging targets for the 1990s, including swift progress towards basic education for all. The Declaration and Framework made only limited reference to education in emergency situations, but war and natural disasters have proved a major barrier to the achievement of EFA. Disasters such as floods, hurricanes and earthquakes have taken a heavy toll of human life, and also of educational opportunity, when they struck densely populated areas. Wars and civil conflicts have left whole nations or regions in poverty and insecurity, and robbed many children and adolescents of the chance to study.

The review of education in emergency situations, presented in this thematic study, shows that displaced and emergency-affected communities make every effort to restore the access of children to schooling. In refugee situations, they are often successful, since host country governments and humanitarian agencies are conscious of their concerns and endeavour to provide the necessary resources. Most refugee camps and settlements have schools, though in some locations they lack textbooks and teachers need additional training and supervision. Internally displaced populations and populations not displaced but suffering from chronic insecurity are less able to access educational resources for their children. In such locations, a generation of children may miss out on basic schooling. In post-conflict situations, the reconstruction of education systems is often delayed. There is wide variability regarding access to secondary and tertiary education, crucial sectors for developing the skilled workforce needed for post-crisis renewal and the transition to national development.

Winder aspects of the Jomtien agenda, such as early childhood development and basic education for adults, have received attention from organisations working for conflict-affected population, notably non-governmental organisations. Pre-school initiatives, literacy classes for youth and adults, notably women, and vocational training have been initiated where humanitarian organisations had access and when funds were available. Likewise there have been initiatives to promote the education and training of children and adults disabled through war, injury by landmines or other causes. There are innovative programmes to promote the education and reintegration of child soldier and ex-combatants.

The thematic study examines some of the new directions in education policy for emergency and post-emergency situations. The 1989 Convention on the Rights of the Child has led to stronger emphasis on the child's right to education. This has coincided with the realisation that rapid educational response helps meet the psychosocial needs of displaced children and communities, leading to the idea that emergency education and recreational supplies should reach affected communities within weeks or not later than three months after a community is displaced. Special policies regarding curriculum may be needed when populations are displaced across national borders and the concept of 'education for repatriation' has taken hold, while there is ongoing exploration of ways to ensure the recognition of studies undertaken by refugees while in exile.

In line with the Jomtien and Beijing emphases on the education of girls and women, there have been efforts to sensitise educators and parents on the importance of girls' education. In some cases, incentives have been provided to help girls attend school, with good results. A multi-faceted strategy adapted to local concerns ad culture is needed. While some aspects of the strategy are cost-free other aspects of the strategy require additional funding, for example to provide sanitary materials and school clothing for older girls, or to support pre-school establishments that free older girls to attend school rather than looking after their younger siblings.

The wide variation in the quality of emergency education reflects uncertainty among supporting agencies about standards for provision of educational materials, in-service teacher training, non-formal education, etc. Appropriate standards of resourcing should be defined and then respected by implementing agencies and donors, with clearer reporting of unmet needs.

The use of new technologies can be a major step forward, especially in situations of chronic instability or when education systems are being rebuilt. Innovative radio programmes such as New Home, New Life for Afghanistan represent a step forward in this area. Education for crisis-affected and post-conflict regions should be included in new international initiatives using electronic and satellite communication technologies.

Education programmes for populations affected by natural disasters or war must be adapted to the special needs of these populations. The *Machel Report on the Impact of Armed Conflict on Children* has led to a greater emphasis on the psychosocial needs of pupils and students, on education for mine awareness and on developing the skills for peace. The devastation caused by AIDS has added a new dimension to the education agenda, since the disease is almost certainly more prevalent in populations where rape may have been used as a tool of war.

Recommendations arising from the study begin with the need to acknowledge the right to education even under conditions of emergency. A systematic effort is needed to publicise the fact that human rights instruments and humanitarian law demand both the protection of children from abuse and under-age recruitment and also the protection of schools in times of war and of the child's right to education. It must be acknowledged again, as in the Jomtien Framework of Action, that resourcing for education in emergency and postcrisis situations 'is an acknowledged international responsibility'.

A key recommendation is that education in emergencies be seen and planned from day one as part of the development process and not solely as a 'relief' effort. Donors should avoid compartmentalisation of funding that can have the effect of creating an uneducated and bitter revenge-oriented generation, because education in the emergency situation was seen as the last call on inadequate 'humanitarian' budgets (for excluded from them). Moreover, restoration of access to schooling in a post-conflict situation should be seen as a funding priority. There should be inter-agency co-ordination to ensure continuity from the early emergency to the reconstruction phase. The task of building a culture of peace to sustain future development in nations and communities divided by ethnic and other conflicts should begin at the emergency stage and continue into the building of civil society in post-conflict situations. Current initiatives in 'education for peace' in the humanitarian context should be brought together on an inter-agency basis, as a contribution to the forthcoming International Decade for a Culture of Peace and Non-Violence for the Children of the World.

Norms and standards should be developed for educational response in natural and man-made catastrophes, with more in-depth field studies by scholars working in the filed of education or regional studies. This includes review and evaluation of modalities of rapid response, and of standards for education in prolonged refugee or crisis situations and for post-conflict reconstruction. There should be review and sharing of educational materials and manuals developed by organisations working in humanitarian emergencies and identification of other materials suited for use in such situations. Training modules on education in emergency and post-conflict situations should be developed for use with staff of humanitarian organisations and as part of standard courses in educational planning.

Inter-agency co-operation and co-ordination in the field of emergency education should be strengthened, and use should be made of the new possibilities of electronic to link field specialists into the inter-agency dialogue.

◆◆◆

Funding Agency Contributions to Education for All

The World Declaration and Framework for Action of the World Conference on Education for All (henceforth 'Jomtien') focused attention on basic education. Agencies were asked to consider ways to assist with basic education through budgetary support, the provision of technical co-operation, revitalised partnerships and a supportive policy context.

This study examines what has happened to funding agency contributions to EFA since Jomtien, focusing on financial contributions to basic education, as well as policy and practice. It is based on the responses to a survey of funding agencies, supplemented by data from the Development Assistance Committee of the Organisation for Economic Co-operation and Development as well as a review of literature.

Agencies vary in their definitions of basic education. In part this variation simply reflects a lack of agreement, but can also be related to their own perceived expertise, their foreign policy goals and their concerns about their status within the agency community. It is also a consequence of the inclusive nature of the consensus reached at Jomtien. Whilst agreement across agencies is neither feasible nor necessary and agreement between agencies and partner countries can be on a bilateral basis, this does pose problems for reporting and comparison, both nationally and internationally.

The data that has been received is described and analysed in Chapter 5, supplemented by data from the Development Assistance Committee. The context is that the overall volume of bilateral aid commitment has dropped in absolute terms during the 1990s (although the high levels at the beginning of the 1990s is partly due to exceptional commitments at the time of the Gulf War). Aid commitments to education as a proportion of overall aid have remained steady at around 15 per cent. For those countries providing disbursements data proportions of overall aid to education have increased over the decade. For multilateral agencies, aid to education has varied throughout the decade, although overall it tends to remain less than 10 per cent. The total absolute volume of bilateral aid commitment to education has remained roughly the same throughout the decade. Multilateral commitments to education rose from $ 1,000m in 1990, to nearly $2,000m in 1994, falling back to $1,300m in 1998.

Bilateral aid commitments to basic education (as a percentage of commitments to all education), have increased from a very low level at the beginning of decade to an average of 25 per cent in the latter part of the decade. For those countries providing disbursement data there has been a similarly dramatic increase. Multilateral aid commitment to basic education (as a proportion of their commitment to the education sector) have been high throughout the 1990s at between 75 per cent and 100 per cent, although disbursements have remained between 30 per cent and 50 per cent. The total value of bilateral aid earmarked for basic education has increased to around $500m at the end of the decade and disbursements (for those countries providing it) have increased from almost zero in 1990 to $170m in 1998. Among multilateral agencies aid commitments to basic education have increased from $550 to an average of $1,500m in the second half of the decade.

Perhaps the main message is the difficulty of collating data not only for this survey but also for the national and international reporting systems that already exist. In part this has been exacerbated by the recent emphasis on joint funding and sector programmes, but there appears also to be a generic problem of accountability that was remarked upon at the beginning of the decade. The situation does not seem to have improved since then.

Jomtien called for targeting of countries and of groups within countries. Based on what agencies have sent us there is a clear commitment to human rights and poverty reduction. Within that overall framework, there does appear to be a focus on basic education (and especially primary education). This has paralleled a focus on Africa and, within that region, a focus on the most highly indebted countries although different agencies do this in different ways. Some other agencies focus on countries 'in transition', others have preferred to concentrate their aid on a small number of countries. However, there has also been the issue of education programmes specifically for marginalised groups. The impact of this targeting on the overall pattern of aid and upon countries in greatest need is less clear, and the implied conditionality may be unhelpful.

Since Jomtien, there has also been an implicit debate over the relative priority as between quantitative expansion to ensure access and efforts to improve quality. On the whole, where formal education has been firmly established for some time the emphasis tends to be on quality and relevance in order to stop parents becoming disillusioned and keeping their children away from school and to avoid disenchantment with education on the whole. Where formal schooling has not been established for such a long time, quality and relevance are indeed essential to attract people but, in addition non-formal solutions are also promoted. Increasingly, the solutions are seen to be context specific so that decentralistion is the key.

Adult education was highlighted as an area of neglect in the Jomtien Declaration. From the documentation we have received, although most of the agencies clam to be involved, the actual level of activity is quite low. Moreover, the impression given is that any involvement is reactive rather than part of a longer term strategy.

Language was another issue raised explicitly in the Jomtien Declaration as having an important effect on access and retention. However, apart from the clear position of UNESCO in favour of the use of mother tongue as the vehicle for as long as possible, very few have a stated policy. Partly this appears to reflect a view that language policy is a political issue on which it is not appropriate for agencies to intervene.

Conventional delivery systems such as projects and programmes are seen to have failed and often not to have been adopted by the host government when funding stopped Instead the emphasis has shifted to policy dialogue and partnership to ensure that aid is used in accordance with host governments policy priorities. Combined with the necessity to take a longer term view of financial sustainability this has led to the progressive adoption/promotion of 'Sector Wide Approaches' by some agencies. However, others are less sure, because of restricted staff, because of difficulties of identifying their own agency contributions, or because the situation in the countries which they aid is not appropriate. From the partner governments' point of view, basket funding has to be handled by a financial system creaking under the strain of managing the current inadequate budgets. Decentralisation simply adds to the complexity of administration. From the agency side, the problem of accountability to their own tax payer is ever present and the more intensive policy dialogue required imposes strains on existing agency staff.

The profile of monitoring and evaluations has been raised over the last decade. Firstly, there have been increasing attempts to introduce assessment and testing procedures into schools in developing countries for monitoring purposes although in practice agencies have resorted to baseline surveys. Secondly, there has been increasing professionalisation in the organisation of evaluation at the agency level, although the time-lines still leaves a lot to be desired.

There appears to have been a conclusive move away from scholarships in the North and, to a lesser but still substantial extent, away from counterpart training via long term TA/TC. The majority of agencies now emphasis institutional capacity building, although exactly what this entails is not always clear. In practice many focus on strengthening the (financial) management and planning systems. There is only limited evidence of successful capacity building throughout the system.

Overall the picture is mixed: a greater emphasis on basic education but within declining commitments overall, clarification of aims and policies but also some divergence, and continuing difficulty in accountability.

◆◆◆

9

Girls' Education

Ten years ago at Jomtien, world leaders committed themselves, in the drive to promote Education for All, to focusing on girls, the largest populations excluded from basic education. The level of awareness of the importance of girls' education has grown significantly, due both to advocacy on the part of communities to international agencies. Over the decade, there have been great improvements in some areas and, unfortunately, reversals in others. Many things have been tried and much is known about what works and what does not in educating girls. New challenges have emerged over the decade. We know that all children have the right to acquire a quality basic education and realistic plans and targets can be put in place for this. During the first decade of the new millennium, stake-holders at all levels, government policy-maker and local school communities, teachers, communities, families and girls themselves need to mobilise resources and get all girls in to school and make it possible for them to complete a basic education. It can be done, it must be done.

This Thematic Study sets out to describe what has been accomplished since 1990; it outlines the major trends, presents the major lessons learned, identifies emerging issues and proposes priorities for the next the to fifteen years.

1. Progress

Since 1990, there has been general acceptance of the critical importance of education to human development and of the key role played by girls' education within this. From a human rights perspective, girls' education must remain a priority as girls still constitute almost two-thirds of the children excluded from basic education. This acceptance has led to commitments in a number of countries around the world and to substantial progress in identifying obstacles to girls' education and in understanding how to overcome these obstacles.

Over the decade, several countries in the Middle East region demonstrated that getting girls into school is quite possible and data from other regions show some encouraging gains. The largest number of girls excluded from basic education remains in South Asia. Sub-Saharan Africa presents the greater challenge, both in terms of the size of the gender gap and because population growth rates remain high and more and more school places are therefore needed. At the same time, sub-Saharan Africa has demonstrated its willingness to try new initiatives and innovations specifically directed at attracting girls to school and keeping them there. Worldwide, discrimination on the basis of gender remains a problem; the focus on girls' education from a gender perspective has also raised important questions about the education of boys.

There have also been some disappointments in the struggle for gender equality in education since Jomtien. In some cases investments in girls' education have, unfortunately, increased rather than decreased the gender gap. In other cases, consistent gains have been halted, or even reversed, due to negative conditions in the environment external to the education system. Lack of adequate data makes it more difficult to accurately assess what is happening to girls in the difficult economic circumstances in parts of Eastern and Central Europe and the Commonwealth of Independent States. Similarly, data are hard to find on the extent of the impact of conflict and external stress on the education of girls in some fifty affected countries.

2. Lessons learned

Most important are the lessons that the decade has given the world, because it is thoughtful and careful application of these lessons on a situation-by-situation basis that will enable acceleration of girls' education so that the target of Education for All can be met within fifteen years. There are many lessons, but they are presented in six general categories for the purpose of summarisation. Girls' education is more than an educational issue. It is deeply influenced by poverty, tradition, habit, legal systems and discrimination—all requiring **political will**, not just to educate girls, but also to eliminate those non-education obstacles.

The evidence is clear; strong and committed **leadership at every level** is essential to put in place the changes that are required to make girls' education a possibility and to maintain the momentum to make it a reality. To be effective, leaders must have sufficient evidence that the changes they are supporting is in the overall best interest of those they are serving. Thus, it becomes important to have **supportive forums** for sharing information and for advocacy. These latter two lessons require up-to-date and practical information derived from an ongoing and serious **research** base that also supports the refinement of existing education data-bases.

These first four categories of lessons are, perhaps, somewhat self-evident. The other two essential areas are less obvious. It is clear that for sustainability and in order to address issues of quality, equivalence, and demand, it is essential to take a **systemic approach** to reforms so that girls are no longer excluded. Finally, in order to ensure that all these areas are adequately pulled together in a coherent way that facilitates the kinds of change required to get all girls into a basic education of good quality, **extended and expanded partnership** are vital. New and creative partnerships have brought the necessary dynamism into education systems, defined broadly, and enabled them to expand and reach out to include girls.

Within each of these categories a wide range of strategies and approaches have been tried. They are not all equally effective and it is clear that some are more applicable to some contexts than others. There have also been some difficult lessons to learn—for example, the discovery that some of the approaches believed to be simple and easily adapted to a wide range of environments are, in fact, quite limited in application.

3. New challenges

Since the Jomtien conference, much has changed and, as a result, new questions and issues have emerged. The Thematic Study selects some of these and shows how they create new and nuanced challenges in the new millennium. Certainly the focus on girls' education from a gender perspective has raised many important issues about boys' education, and it is fully recognised that a **gender-sensitive education** is one of the things that will make the vision of Education for All a reality. Similarly, the evaluation over the decade in girls' education and, in particular, attempts to better understand the gender gap have resulted in a much better understanding of **exclusion**—from school, but also within the school, in the classroom itself, exclusion from effective learning. This work, often pioneered by a focus on girls, can make it possible to adapt what is known to include other excluded and marginalised groups.

It is very apparent from the work in girls' education that access to and quality of education are inextricably linked—it would be easier if this were not the case. This bears very closely on two other critical aspects of girls' (and boys') education: the need to understand both demand and supply, and how these play out, one against the other. Everybody agrees that quality is important, but the experience of and challenge arising from girls' education is that the very **notion of quality must change** in some very fundamental ways. A quality education includes learning the basics and learning how to learn in a safe, secure, gender-sensitive, healthy and protective learning environment. This finding presents an enormous challenge to systems that often find it difficult to offer basic education meeting the conventional definition of quality.

A challenge that is not discussed much, but is emerging, is a worldwide growing push from forces in support of religious fundamentalism. Often this results in a decrease in, rather than increase in, the rights and empowerment of girls and women. This links of fundamentalism to partriarchy and their implications for educational change deserve more attention if girls' education is to move ahead at an accelerated pace.

Understanding these challenges and monitoring how they are affecting girls' education require more robust data that extend beyond the conventional education statistics. They also demand **disaggregated data** so that the nature of challenges can be properly understood.

4. Priorities

It is not possible to address all issues simultaneously. Priorities have to be set—some can be set globally, but good analysis at local and national levels is critical to determine how best to overcome the barriers to girls' education in a timely manner. Simple **access** to any kind of basic education remains a major issue for millions of children, the majority of them girls.

Careful and strategic application of lessons learned to **close and gender gap** and **address educational quality** are essential if *all* are to receive a quality basic education. There is no single intervention that will work everywhere—each context/action will have to be adapted to the particular and nuanced circumstances that are working against girls' education. Linked to this is the fact that efforts in support of girls' education must move from what are primarily limited efforts to go to massive scale. This will present enormous challenges around the world, but without such an effort, the majority of excluded girls will remain on the outside looking in for the foreseeable future.

To make this extra, to accelerate progress, will require ingenuity, persistence, ongoing fostering of new partnership, and significant resource mobilisation and utilisation. There are probably fewer 'lessons learned' in girls' education with regard to resource mobilisation than any of the other areas selected for discussion. Yet this topic may present one of the greatest remaining challenges that must be met in the years to come.

◆◆◆

10

Inclusion in Education: Participation of Disabled Learners

1. Introduction: making progress in inclusive education!

Overview

This study reviews developments in the theory, policy and practice of inclusive education since the Jomtien Conference. It has a dual focus. Firstly, it examines progress in the development of an inclusive system of education which, in responding to the diversity of learners, minimises exclusion for all. Secondly, within this broad task, it charts the progress made by learners with impairments in overcoming barriers of access to, and participation in, education.

The study contains analysis interspersed with examples of instructive practice. Such practice illustrates barriers to inclusive development encountered at all levels of the system, and ways that have been found to surmount them. It provides a survey of changes in practice and has a strategic function in identifying priorities for development.

Including learners with impairments

Inclusive education is commonly associated with the mainstream participation of learners with impairments and those categorised as having 'special educational needs'. Throughout the past decade, learners with impairments continued to be disproportionately excluded from any form of education, particularly in countries of the South. They remain the group most likely to be left out of the agenda when educational exclusion is discussed.

Learners with impairments are not a homogeneous group. They are as different from—and similar to—one another as any learner is different from—and similar to the other. No two learners are exactly alike. For example, learners who are deaf and whose first language is sign language have a need for a sign language community which has to be reflected in plans for increasing their participation in education.

The study builds on the success of the United Nations Standard Rules on the Equalisation of Opportunities, the World Declaration on Education for All and the Salamanca Statement and Framework for Action in highlighting the exclusion of disabled people at all levels of education and society, and the formidable obstacles to participation that they still face. It recognises the key role that has been placed by organisations of disabled people and parents of disabled children in pushing for the recognition of the right to education of disabled learners in their neighbourhood. It documents what has been learnt about the barriers to the inclusion of learners with impairments and how these can be overcome, and the role of governments and non-governmental organisations in supporting their education . In most countries of the world there are examples of instructive practice of the inclusion of learners with impairments even where economic circumstances or priorities lead to large classes and poor physical conditions.

From the inclusion of learners with impairment to learning and participation for all

However, in this study inclusive education is not only concerned with learners with impairments but with overcoming the barriers to the learning and participation experienced by all learners vulnerable to exclusion from full educational participation.

The view of inclusion within the study involves a shift of focus from learners to learning centres, education systems and societies. It is about creating inclusive cultures, policies and practices at all levels of the system. The educational inclusion of any group of learners cannot proceed very far without developing the capacity of learning centres to respond to learner diversity. This step, moving beyond access to learning centres for some learners to the development of quality education for all, is perceived in many countries as critical to the development of their education policies, requiring a transformation of traditional approaches to teaching and learning. Inclusive education is thus seen as a means by which educational development can take place. By employing a restricted view of inclusive education, interventions have limited their contribution to sustainable educational development.

Links to other thematic studies

The study is a companion to the thematic studies addressing 'children in difficult circumstances', 'gender inequality', 'refugees' and 'excluded learners', At the policy and administrative levels, the thematic study on decentralisation and community participation is seen to address some of the critical factors in the development of inclusive learning centres. It also has close links with the studies on 'health and nutrition'. The development of inclusion in education involves attention to the conditions which encourage learning for all both inside and outside learning centres.

2. Developing conceptions of inclusive education

An approach to inclusion in education

Inclusion in education is an unending process. It involves increasing the participation of learners in and reducing their exclusion from the cultures, curricula and communities of local learning centres. It requires the restructuring of the cultures, policies and practices in schools so that they support the learning and participation of the diversity of learners in their community. A concern with overcoming barriers to the access and participation of particular learners may reveal gaps in the attempts of a school to respond to diversity more generally. Diversity is not viewed as a problem to be overcome by attempting to separate learners into groups, homogeneous in background and attainment. Diversity is seen instead as cause for celebration and as a rich resource for teaching and learning. All learners are seen as having a right to an education in their locality. Inclusion is concerned with fostering a mutually sustaining relationship between schools and communities. Inclusion in education is one aspect of inclusion in society.

Barriers to learning and participation

The concept of 'special educational needs' is not used in this study except in referring to work of others who use the term. The term is not seen as helpful in resolving educational difficulties and is a barrier to the development of inclusive practice. Furthermore, it encourages educators to attribute difficulties in education to deficits in learners.

The study adopts the notion of 'barriers to learning and participation'. It asks: What barriers to learning exist at each level of the education systems? Who experiences barriers to learning and participations? How can barriers to learning and participation be minimised? What are the resources that can be mobilised to support learning and participation at each level of the education system?

Learners who experience barriers to learning and participation include learners in poverty, those affected by war and environmental degradation and change, learners who are victims of abuse and violence, street children, children being brought up outside of their own families, children in abusive forms of child labour, learners with impairments, girls in situations where their education is seen as less important than that of boys, learners affected by HIV and AIDS or other chronic illness, nomadic learners, learners from oppressed groups and subjected to racism or other forms of discrimination, girls who are pregnant or have young children, learners whose home language is different from the language of instruction, etc.

A 'social model' of difficulties in learning and disability

The use of the concept of 'barriers to learning and participation' for the difficulties that learners encounter implies a social model of difficulties in learning and disability. A social model of disability has been strongly advocated by organisations of disabled people around the world but its implications for understanding difficulties experienced by learners in education have been less explored. According to the model, barriers to learning and participation arise through an interaction between learners and their contexts: the people, policies, institutions, cultures, social and economic circumstances that affect their lives.

Disabilities are barriers to participation for people with impairments or chronic illness. Impairments can be defined as a long-term 'limitation of physical or mental or sensory function'. Disabilities are created by the interaction of discriminatory attitudes, actions, cultures, policies and institutional practices with impairments, pain or chronic illness. While we may often be able to do little to overcome the impairments of learners, we can have a considerable impact in overcoming the physical, personal and institutional barriers to their access and participation.

Measuring the progress of inclusion

It is easier to measure the progress of inclusion when we use a narrow definition of it than when we adopt a broad one. It is relatively straightforward to work out what proportion of learners with impairments in an area attend schools or whether they attend a mainstream or a special school, though even such statistics imply a regular and accurate gathering of statistics and an agreed definition of impairment. However, it is far more complicated to provide an assessment of improvement in the quality of the social and academic participation of learners in learning centres, or of overall changes in the balance between pressures for inclusion and exclusion at all levels of an education system. Nevertheless we cannot allow a wish to gather simple statistics to determine our approach to inclusion.

3. Developing inclusive education policies

Power and influence in policy development

Many governments, organisations and individuals have been influenced by the strong stance of international organisations on inclusive education, particularly the Jomtien Declaration and the Salamanca Statement. The latter argued that 'the development of inclusive schools as the most effective means for achieving education for all must be recognised as a key government policy and accorded a privileged place on the nation's development agenda'.

The importance of clear international and national policies is widely advocated. Yet in many cases the implications of national policy for local practice are not spelled out and implementation remains patchy. It is increasingly recognised that policy development has to operate at all levels. Developments within communities have to be supported by local and national policies. National policies have to engage with the realities of life within local communities and ensure that strategies are in place to move local practice forward. There is increasing recognition too of the harmony that is required between non-governmental organisations, and between them and national, local government administrations and local community and religious organisations. The significant role of religious organisations in providing education in many countries is sometimes overlooked by international agencies.

In many countries there is a large private sector catering for the more privileged communities, with the state providing a basic education in the poorest areas. Such education is generally seen as having a low value and this is a major excluding pressure which it is extremely difficult to combat. Such divisions may also be culturally entrenched. According to one group of contributors to this review, in their region: 'the idea of exclusive education is more entrenched than inclusive education' Educational inclusion is revealed as part of a political process which pears on the distribution of wealth and opportunity in society.

An emphasis on rights to inclusion in education of learners with impairments has been pushed forward by disabled people's organisations and by organisations of parents of disabled children sometimes in alliance with each other. This is similar to the ways which women's organisations and ethnic organisations have championed the rights to equal treatment of girls and boys, and all ethnic groups. Where the proportion of learners with impairments attending a local school has increased, frequently this has been as a result of a struggle between parents and professionals: The assertion of rights by parents of learners with impairments and disabled people, drawing on the influence of international organisations, has had a major effect on policy development. The Standard Rules on the Equalisation of Opportunities for Persons with Disabilities, the Convention on the Rights of the Child and the Salamanca Statement and Framework for Action have had an impact on these developments.

Developing national policy

In most countries the division between special and general education policy clouds the development of inclusion policy. Inclusion policy is often seen as part of special needs education policy and this prevents an examination of the exclusionary pressures within the system as a whole and undermines the development of inclusion. In countries of the North, in particular, inclusion policy may be sub-divided into policies concerned with the inclusion of learners who have impairments or are categorised as having special educational needs, and policies about reducing social disadvantage called 'social inclusion' policies.

Some countries have adopted an approach to raising attainment levels in learning centres which encourages them to compete against each other for positions on league tables of educational attainments. Parents compete, too, to get their children into the most desired learning centres, and the most successful schools choose the parents and learners they prefer. Such policies put an additional pressure on learners in economically poor areas because they lead to a concentration of the most vulnerable learners in particular learning centres which may be forced to close as numbers and general attainment levels fall. An inclusive approach to raising standards is about providing the support necessary to enable schools to encourage the highest achievements of all learners in their neighbourhood.

In systems attempting to become responsive to learner diversity, there are attempts to introduce flexibleand responsive assessment policies. The practice of grade repetions arising from applying single grades for particular ages is being questioned, along with forms of tracking or streaming. These practices are based on the assumption that teaching groups need to be as homogeneous as possible. In contrast to this approach, inclusion involves valuing diversity in teaching groups and the adaptation of teaching approaches to support them. (see chapters 4 and 5).

Inappropriate curricula, taught by teachers poorly prepared to teach the learners infront of them, remain wdespread and major causes of student absenteeism, failure and drop out. For many learners the language of instruction is inaccessible. Policy has to be directed at creating conditions for active, successful learning within all learning centres.

Legislation specifying national curricula and assessment systems must take account of the range of attainments of similar age learners if they are to be used to support inclusive practice. Many countries have enacted laws giving access to the education system to learners irrespective of the severity of an impairment (educability laws) and many have also passed legislation indicating a presumption that this education should take place in a regular rather than a special school. Some make distinction between severe and less severe impairment with the presumption of special school education in the first case. In very few cases does the law come close to giving a right to an education within the local community school.

There is an on-going debate between those who want a single inclusive system and those who wish to maintain a separate special needs education system. All countries are faced with the challenge of addressing diversity amongst the learner population. To date, no system has avoided or made a complete shift away from segregated thinking about learners with impairments. Even in contexts where education is provided in the mainstream, this has often produced segregating practices inside regular learning centres.

In some countries the special system has been the only means for distributing targeted resources for learners with impairments. Inclusive funding strategies involve a combination of devolving funds to learning centres to respond to diversity generally and providing funds on an area basis for equipment and specialist support, and advice for a small number of learners with very severe impairments. This system has to be monitored to ensure that funds are directed to reducing the particular barriers to learning and participation in the neighbourhood.

Learning from countries of the North and the South

Caution has to be exercised in applying the solutions to educational problems that are adopted in one country in an entirely different context. For example, special needs education arose in countries of the North in the context of universal, free education. Where countries of the South adopt the special school model as the way to include learners with impairments in the education system, in the absence of universal education and without a widespread belief that such learners have a right to education, only a minority of learners with impairments receive an education and these generally belong to privileged sections of society.

Yet, countries of the North and the South do have much to learn from each other. Many educators in countries of the North suggest that inclusion cannot move forward because of the limitation of resources in their countries. Yet, there are examples of creative inclusive practices within countries of the South, in the context of severely limited resources. Such examples reveal the importance of shared inclusive cultures and values in enabling progress.

4. Developing inclusive learning centres

Taking education to communities

State primary and secondary education is generally school based. However, non-governmental organisations and others are involved in improvising education with groups who do not have access to schools or have a life-stye for which schools are not the immediate solution. Such groups may include street children, other children who work from economic necessity and nomadic learners. Education cannot be identified solely with schooling.

Improving the conditions for learning

Many learners face barriers to learning and participation within learning centres because of poor nutrition or a supportive environment at home, the absence of basic resources such as water and sanitation, learning resources such as books and paper, the preparation, commitment and attitudes of staff and the relevance and accessibility of the curriculum and buildings. Many learners arrive at learning centres unable to concentrate because of hunger or tired from a long trek or work. In some placed, both in countries of the North and South, the security of buildings is a problem and it is difficult to keep any equipment on the learning centre premises. Such difficulties can be reduced when communities feel ownership of their local learning centres.

In most countries there are instructive attempts to increase the participation of learners. In learning centres attempting to become more inclusive, the development of a supportive community for staff and learners is seen as important as the encouragement of academic attainment. The basis for sustainable development within any learning centre is the emergence of an inclusive culture, underpinned by shared values, that can be passed on to new members of the centre's community. The development of a safe, secure, accepting, collaborating, stimulating community in which everyone is valued becomes the basis for encouraging the achievement of all learners. It involves making all learners, parents/carers and community members, welcome and valuing them all equally. There is a concern to uncover and minimise barriers to learning and participation in all areas of the centre and to remove all forms of discrimination.

Producing inclusive learning centre policies

In order to plan to increase inclusion, learning centres have to identify barriers to learning and participation within any aspects of their work and may construct policies to minimise them. The precise nature of these policies depends on the characteristics of a particular area. Inclusive education involves staff as well as learners. It is necessary to ensure that all staff appointments and promotions are carefully considered and with an attempt to make the teaching staff representative of the communities of the learners. Staff tries to ensure that buildings are accessible to learners with impairments. There may be policies for recruiting new learners from the surrounding area, reducing barriers to their attendance, and procedures for making all new learners and all new staff feel settled. Policies may need to be in place to minimise bullying between any members of the centre community.

There is considerable variation in the support that is available for staff and learners and how it is used. Inclusive support can be defined as all those activities which increase the capacity of the staff in learning centres to respond to the diversity of their learners. All staff development activities and any support policies need to have this as an aim, which needs to be shared with support agencies external to the school with the help of local educational administrations.

Evolving inclusive teaching and learning practices

With the support of staff development activities, learning centres attempting to become more inclusive increase the responsiveness of lessons to the diversity of learners. The curriculum itself can foster an understanding of difference. Sometimes particular arrangements have to be made so the learners are not disadvantaged because their home language is different from the language used for teaching. Teachers have to try to ensure that the words they use are understood by learners or are explained to them. The details of inclusive teaching strategies differ depending on available resources but the principles are constant: learning and teaching are varied and differentiated, collaborative, active and draw on all available resources within teachers and other staff, learners, parents/carers and committees.

All learning centres and their communities have resources to support education that are not fully mobilised. The lower the staffing levels and material resources, the more important it becomes to release the potential in under-used resources in the school and in the surrounding community. The diversity of learners is itself a rich resource for learning. Every learner, irrespective of his or her attainment or impairment, is also a teacher. There are examples of learning centres employing the difference between learners in terms of maturity and skills to enhance learning opportunities. The Child-do-Child approach draws on children to act as resource for their communities. Parents of all learners have a deep knowledge about their children and this can be particularly valuable for children and young people whose learning becomes a focus of concern, such as some learns with impairments. There are learning opportunities with all communities which can be exploited for education.

Indices for inclusion

In several countries, indices of inclusion have been developed to assess participation in schools and to assist schools in planning inclusive development. Most of these indices have concentrated on learners with impairments, though they have carried the assumption that enabling schools to respond effectively to one aspect of diversity will help them to become good places for all learners. One group of researchers drew on these earlier attempts but with a change in emphasis so that the index is concerned with the inclusive development of the whole school for staff as well as learners and their parents/ carers. It consists of a set of materials which support staff to share their existing knowledge, engage in a detailed examination of the exclusionary pressures and inclusionary possibilities in all aspects of their school/learning centre. It requires them to draw on the views of learners, parents, community members and other stake-holders in education locally.

5. Developing human resources to support inclusion

The development of inclusive capacity

In systems undergoing inclusive development, change has to be introduced at all levels and sectors of the system if it is not to be undermined. Those in government directing change must have detailed knowledge of their education system and of educational developments. While teacher educators play a vital role in encouraging more inclusive, flexible and responsive ways of working, they also carry teaching and academic traditions which may support a less inclusive system of education. Some may find that qualifications gained in other countries have not prepared them sufficiently for their own educational realities. They may have grown up in relatively affluent urban circumstances, amongst communities unfamiliar with the rural conditions and cultures of many learners. They too need to be introduced to new thinking in order to overcome their own prejudices about excluded learns in general and learners with impairments in particular.

Revising initial teacher education

In many countries the teaching force is not representative of the ethnic groups, linguistic communities and impairments within the population, and this requires a concerted strategy and monitoring. For many teachers the content of their training remains unrelated to the nature of the teaching job and the conditions in which they work; there is a separation between theory and practice. Inclusive initial teacher education requires methods which are themselves inclusive. In some teacher education institutions in both the North and South, teacher educators attempt to teach a content about active learning in diverse classrooms using passive methods which take no account of the prospective teachers' backgrounds and experiences. On many teacher-education courses, inclusion is considered in separate sessions, usually associated with learners with impairments or those categorised as having 'special educational needs', rather than permeating the approach to education in all courses.

In most countries a rigid separation continues to be maintained between special and mainstream teacher education and this discourages the development of inclusive teaching approaches. In some cases the qualifications do not permit specialist teachers to teacher regular classes. There has been a growing recognition that any specialism should follow a common general training.

Encouraging staff development

Staff development activities are most successful when they are linked to whole school improvement. Cascade models of training, which attempt to multiply the effect of limited training resources, require groups of teachers from one learning centre to train together, supported by the head teacher, if they are to be enabled to effect changes in their practice and spread these changes to other institutions. Arranging learning centres in clusters widens the resources available for training and dissemination. Clusters could include special and mainstream centres sharing resources as a step towards greater inclusion. The knowledge of parents and disabled people can form an effective part of staff and school development. In many countries teaching assistants are employed sometimes to support learners with impairments. There needs to be clear strategies for how these staff can support the learning and participation of all learners. This may involve some separate training but involvement of all staff in shared training activities provides the best model for collaboration.

UNESCO's *Teacher Education Resource Pack: Special Needs in the Classroom* has been particularly influential in encouraging inclusive learning centre development in eighty countries. It involves teachers in a set of activities which give them experience of collaborative, inclusive teaching and learning strategies and help them to incorporate these within their own thinking and practice. Despite its name it discourages the division of learners into these with and without 'special needs'. It supports teachers in sharing and reflecting on their experience, and drawing on the recorded and observed experience of others, in order to teach diverse groups together.

Providing support for diversity

Countries differ greatly in the extent to which they have invested in specialists for learners who experience difficulties. These include teachers for particular categorised groups of learners with impairments, educational psychologists, speech therapists, occupational therapists, sign language interpreters and interpreters for those who do not speak the languages used in the school/learning centre. In countries of the South, widespread employment of highly trained professionals may be prohibitively expensive, and unavailable at times, and thus community expensive, and unavailable at times, and thus community-based support has to be constructed from people available in the education service and in the communities. In countries of the North and the South, if support is to be used efficiently, its role in increasing the capacity of learning centres to respond to diversity, has to be recognised. It has to be based as close to learning centres as possible and to employ a social model of difficulties in learning. The support coming from specialist centres will need to adjust and match the new setting compatible with inclusive development.

6. Challenges and opportunities

From access to participation

In many countries there is a recognition that providing access to a local learning centre is only the first stage in overcoming the exclusion from education of learners. It may not be the most difficult step, even though there are many examples where the presence of a previously excluded learner acts as a catalyst for the improvement of teaching and learning for all students. The crucial stages involve a shift of perspective and values from the denial to the celebration of diversity and then the systematic fostering of high quality teaching and learning opportunities for all learners.

Learning from experience

There is a growing experience in many countries of how barriers to learning and participation can be identified and reduced. This experience is a rich resource to support inclusive development. However, many people find it difficult to learn from the experience of others. They can see experience as invalid if it is gained in different circumstances, in different countries, or in different areas of the same country. Enabling educators to adopt a critical, reflective view of their own practice so that they can absorb lessons from the instructive practice of others, remains a major challenge for those initiating change in education systems and learning centres.

Ending policy fragmentation

Inclusive education is not a new initiative with an associated set of policies that are additional to existing educational activities. It is not a form of special needs education but an alternative to it. It is concerned with the appropriate response to all aspects of diversity within the mainstream, in which learners with impairments are one important element. The continuation of separate special needs education policies represents one of the challenges to the development of inclusive approaches to teaching and learning.

In all countries there is a tendency for new labels to be given to educational initiatives associated with particular government departments or non-governmental organisations rather than to connect them with existing policies. Non-governmental organisations may find themselves in competition with each other to provide services and these services can be poorly integrated with State provision. In some areas despite an overall shortage of resources there are more interventions than the system can effectively absorb. While policy fragmentation and overlapping interventions are wasteful of resources in countries of the North, they have particularly serious consequences for economically poorer nations. There is a need to bring together educational policies under the label such as 'community-based rehabilitation', 'social inclusion and exclusion', 'special needs education', 'health promoting schools', 'child-friendly schools' within the Education for All framework so that education for all is truly concerned with providing a high quality education for all learners within their local communities.

Inclusion and sustainable development

Involvement in education is an expression of hope for future generations. The Education for All movement recognises that the exclusion from full participation in education, experienced by any individual, is a global responsibility. In every region of the world, there are examples of practice inspired by inclusive values, at all levels of the system. Yet for people uprooted by environmental change, in the middle of violent conflict or recovering from its effects, living in continuing poverty, or in regions suffering rapid economic decline, inclusive educational development can seem remote. In many respects, education is less inclusive, globally, than it was at the time of the Jomtien Conference. In such circumstances, educational interventions have to be carefully directed.

Removing exclusion in and from education is only part of the process of reducing exclusion in society. It cannot be separated from policies for economic development and employment. Sustainable inclusive educational development has to be linked to the building of sustainable working opportunities in sustainable environments.

The need to think inclusively in education, as in other areas of society, has never been more important. The mobility of people within and between countries has made human diversity more widely apparent. There have been many painful reminders in the last decade of the threat to peace and stability that occurs when diversity ceases to be valued. As argued by the International Commission on Education for the Twenty-First Century, chaired by Jacques Delors, in adopting 'a regard for diversity' as a fundamental principle and in 'combating all forms of exclusion' from education, we can restore education to its 'central place as a melting-pot' contribution to social harmony.

Inclusive thinking is a reminder that education must be as concerned with the sustenance of communities, as with personal achievement and national economic performance. It allows us to recognise the undermining effects on social cohesion and the consequent economic costs of a narrow technical focus in education, where the sole concern is with 'what works' to increase average school attainment, narrowly conceived in terms of academic results. Inclusive education provides a route to educational development that is morally and hence technically sustainable because it provides a reasoned basis for action in international organisation, governments, non-governmental organisation, communities and learning centres.

A comment on terms:

Disability: a barrier to participation of people with impairments or chronic illness arising from an interaction of the impairment or illness with discriminatory attitudes, actions, cultures, policies or institutional practices.

Impairment: a limitation of physical, intellectual or sensory function.

Inclusive cultures: the shared practices and values within a community that support and sustain the widening of membership of that community.

Learner: children and young people eligible for primary and secondary education, who may or may not be in a school.

Learning centre: a place where learners are educated together, including schools and less formal arrangements.

Participation: the shared engagement in learning and social activities with others in such a way as to foster a sense of belonging to the group.

◆◆◆

Literacy and Adult Education

1. Introduction

The 1990 World Conference on Education for All (WCEFA), Jomtien, Thailand, included adult literacy as one of its six major worldwide goals. Specifically, a number of national educational goals related to youth and adult education were agreed upon, including; (1) to reduce the number of adult illiterates to half of the 1990 level by the year 2000; and (2) to improve learning achievement to an agreed percentage of a appropriate age cohort (which might vary from country to country). As part of all Jomtien goals, a new approach to learning was emphasised, one that focused on measurable learning achievement (rather than mere class attendance or participation). These challenges, then, have formed the basis for much of renewed international interest in literacy and adult education over the past decade and, in many ways, remain the continuing Jomtien challenge for the first quarter of the new millennium.

While the complete elimination of illiteracy by the year 2000 was adopted as a goal of UNESCO and a significant number of its member states in the Udaipur Declaration of two decades ago, the Jomtien Conference scaled back such promises, and chose a more modest, and theoretically achievable, goal of cutting illiteracy rates in half by the year 2000. The reasons for this reduction in targeted goal were numerous. As this report will describe, important gains have been made in literacy and adult education over the past decade since Jomtien—in various places and using various methods—but the overall literacy situation remains still today one of the major challenges of the twenty-first century.

Over the 1990s, views on literacy and illiteracy have changed dramatically. Many literacy specialists and policy-makers have moved away from the monolithic view of illiteracy as a disease in which the germs might be 'eradicated' with an appropriate drug or vaccination. Rather, literacy is now more broadly accepted as a product of educational, social and economic factors that cannot be radically changed in short periods of time. Indeed, while numerous efforts have been undertaken in both research and practice in the past decade, it comes as no surprise that the fundamental problems and the global statistics on literacy have changed only moderately, whether in industrialised or developing countries, Nonetheless, due in large part to increasingly competitive and knowledge based economies across the world, most governments and international/bilateral agencies have expressed increased concern about illiteracy and low literacy since Jomtien, even though resource allocations have remained at a disproportionately small fraction of what is contributed to formal schooling.

The present global thematic study on literacy and adult education considers trends and innovations that have been particularly salient over the WCEFA decade, though many of these same issues have been present during the preceding decades. The particular focus here is on the knowledge base that is currently available as well as the gaps that need to be filled in order for the field to make substantial progress in the coming decade and beyond. The 'bottom line' of this study is that the overlapping fields of literacy and adult education can and must do much better in the future, but will require not only more fiscal resources, but professional expertise (including teachers, specialists programmes directors and policy-makers) as well.

2. Concepts and definitions

Many countries have been actively striving to achieve Jomtien's major goal of meeting the basic learning needs for all children, youth and adults, as well as the conjoint necessity for an adequate methodology for understanding whether such goals are being met. Current national and international capacities remain limited, however, for a variety of historical reasons. In the literacy domain, there is a long tradition of statistics gathering, but due to changing definitions of literacy, as well as a dearth of human capacity in the educational measurement field, the data on literacy have long been open to question and debate.

Many definitions exist for literacy. All relate in some way, at their core, to an individuals ability to understand printed text and to communicate through print. Most contemporary definitions portray literacy in relative rather than absolute terms. They assume that there is not single level of skill or knowledge that qualifies a person as 'literate', but rather that there are multiple levels and kinds of literacy (e.g., numeracy technological literacy). In order to have bearing on real life situations, definitions of literacy must be sensitive to skills needed in *out-of-school* contexts, as well as to school-based competencies.

Historically, it was possible to make an arbitrary distinction between those who had been to school and those who had not; this was especially obvious in the newly independent countries of the developing world, which were just beginning to provide public schooling beyond a relatively small elite. Those who had been to school were labeled as 'literate'. However, this situation has changed dramatically. While there are still millions of adults who have never attended school in even the poorest countries of the world the majority of the population in the two youngest generations (up to about age 40) has received some schooling. While this leaves open the serious question of the level of literacy of this perhaps minimally-schooled population, it nonetheless points to a world with a much more variegated landscape of literacy skills, levels of achievement and degree of regular use.

Jomtien influenced the definitional aspect of the literacy goal by broadening the discussion to that of, basic learning needs or competencies, which are seen not only in terms of mastery of the 3 R's (reading, writing and arithmetic), but also in terms of other knowledge, problem-solving and life skills. Together, basic learning needs or competencies are thought to promote empowerment and access to a rapidly changing world. They should support independent functioning and coping with practical problems or choices as a parent or worker or citizen, and are seen as critical gatekeeper to job entry and societal advancement in all countries. Thus, when defining basic learning needs or competencies, there is a need to refer both to formal school-based skills (such as ability to read prose text or to understand mathematical notations) and also the ability to manage functional tasks and demands, regardless of whether such competencies were developed through formal or non-formal education, or through personal experiences in diverse informal learning situations. The challenge of changing definitions is not a trivial one and will influence not only how policy-makers view literacy goals, but also how programme developers will seek to promote literacy and adult education in the twenty-first century.

3. Status and trends in literacy statistics

In order to provide worldwide statistical comparisons, international agencies have relied almost entirely on data provided by its member countries. According to the most recent UNESCO statistics (and estimates), world literacy rates have been dropping over the past two to three decades, apparently due primarily to increase in primary school enrolments. Yet these data also indicate that the actual numbers of illiterates have remained relatively constant, due to population growth. It was once assumed that increased efforts for achieving universal primary schooling would lead to a drop toward zero in adult illiteracy around the world. These optimistic views are no longer widely believed, for a variety of reasons including: continued increases in population growth in developing countries; declining quality of basic education where rapid expansion has taken place; upward changes in the skill standards for literacy both in developing and industrialised countries; improved measurement of literacy through surveys which show that previous estimates of literacy based on school grade achieved often overestimate actual basic learning competencies.

According to UNESCO, there were an estimated 894 million illiterates in the world in 1990, an estimated 887 million in 1995 and an estimated 8975 million in 2000. Of these illiterates, the majority are women, in some countries accounting for up to two-thirds of adult illiteracy. Regionally eastern and southern Asia have the highest number of illiterates, with an estimated 68 per cent of the worlds' total illiterate population. Sub-Saharan Africa and the Arab States have about the same (40 per cent) adult illiteracy rate, with Latin America at about half this rate. Overall, the geographic distribution of adult illiterates has not changed very much over the Jomtien decade (or over the past several decades). However, it should be noted that comparisons of illiteracy rates in developing and industrialised countries can be misleading, since definitions of literacy and illiteracy now vary widely, and the UNESCO statistics on industrialised countries are no longer seen by OECD countries as applicable. One consequence of these changes in standards (and the international surveys that have been done in recent years) it that adult literacy has become, during the Jomtien decade, a greatly increased policy interest in OECD countries. Policy interest in literacy in developing countries remains high, but competition for resources has remained a major impediment.

4. Domains of innovation

Innovations are central to future success in literacy and adult education, and learner motivation, once access is achieved, is a key dimension for any programmatic improvement. This is true whether one is in Bangladesh or in Bolivia. A major problem consistently mentioned by service-providers and policy-makers is that participation levels drop off rapidly after the first weeks or months of programme participation. Many varied and valid reasons have been cited as causes of this problem, such as: inadequate programme quality; lack of time and resources of learners; poor quality of textbooks and pedagogy; lack of social marketing; and so forth. There is little doubt, however, that the general factor behind all of these technical issues is that learners, for whatever sets of reasons, do not feel motivated to participate and remain in such voluntary programmes.

Innovative ways of meeting learner needs while at the same time enhancing learner motivation include: language policy and planning (e.g., providing more robust methods for introducing mother-tongue and second language literacy), empowerment and community participation (e.g., decentralisation of literacy provision through non-governmental organisations), learning, instruction and materials design (e.g., better concatenation in materials development and production between formal and non-formal education domains), gender and family (e.g. further growth of intergenerational, mother-child literacy programmes), multi-sectoral connections (e.g. adapting literacy instruction for integration with health education and agricultural extension programmes), post-literacy and income-generation (e.g., integration of literacy with income generation schemes), technology and distance education (e.g., use of multimedia for improved teacher training). Case examples of developments in each of these areas are provided in the study.

5. Capacity-building, professional development and external agency support

Capacity-building is at the heart of the renewal of effective and high quality work in literacy and adult education. The committed involvement of professionals is required for any system wide change. One major limitation for change in adult literacy is that the large majority of the instructional staff is part-time (including volunteers with high turnover). Furthermore, there have been only limited resources and strategies for involving full-time professionals as well as volunteer and part-time instructors and tutor in meaningful professional development. There is a major need to develop systems and capacities that enable administrators, teachers and tutors to engage in professional staff training and development as an ongoing process within programmes and to link staff development more closely with service improvement and evaluation/monitoring. Teachers and administrators should have more opportunities to understand and learn from local problems and to invent local solutions. Increasing the proportion of full-time instructors is an essential element of enhanced professional development; without more full-time staff, programmes have little incentive to spend scarce resources on professional development.

Many agencies, bilateral and multilateral, provide support for literacy and adult education, but only UNESCO has put literacy in its top list of educational priorities over recent decades. The UNESCO Institute for Education in Hamburg, which organised CONFINTEA V in 1997, and the International Literacy Institute—a UNESCO partner, which organised the World Conference on Literacy (Philadelphia, 1996) and a series of regional forums on literacy, have helped UNESCO's international agenda in literacy and adult education. In addition, UNDP, UNICEF and the World Bank have supported adult literacy programmes over the decades, along with a number of key bilateral agencies. As part of its Education Sector Review (1997), the World Bank, in collaboration with

Norway, recently began an important initiative on adult basic education and literacy in Africa. Various evaluation projects have been commissioned such as in Uganda, and projects in Ghana, Senegal, Gambia and elsewhere are underway or in planning. UNDP was active in the 1960s and 1970s with the Experimental World. Literacy Programme, and UNICEF remains active in promoting basic skills and life skills for out of school youths (particularly girls and young women).

6. Challenges for the future

Literacy and adult education will need to focus more than ever before on which *kinds* and what level of literacy are required for each society, as well as for specific groups within that society. The year 2000 international statistics, dramatic as they remain, do not fully reveal the endemic problems associated with adult literacy work. The central problem, with the broader field of education, is the *quality* of the education as it relates to the *individual* adult learner. National campaigns and programmes have often gone wrong because of the need for too rapid progress and for economies of scale. This combination of factors has led to low motivation on the part of adult learners around the world, and to poor outcomes in both learning achievement and participation rates. What is needed is a greater focus on programme quality along the following themes: professional development, learner motivation, knowledge-based programme design and increased openness to new approaches. Each of these challenges is described very briefly below.

Professional development. The professional development of administrators, directors, teachers and tutors is an ongoing and critical process for programme improvement in literacy and adult education. Teachers and administrators should have more opportunities to investigate local problems and to invent local solutions. Increasing the proportion of full-time instructors is an essential element of enhanced professional development; indeed, without more full-time staff, programmes have little incentive to spend scarce resources on professional development.

Learner motivation. The motivation of adult learners is a key dimension that either can promote participation and retention, or, when lacking, can lead to poor take up and retention of literacy and adult education programmes. In contrast to what was thought over recent decades, the challenge of motivation lies not in providing the 'political will' of governments, but rather in finding ways to provide what the private sector terms, rather simply, 'customer service'. Thus, in order to reach the unreached and the most excluded (e.g., unschooled, women, ethnic-linguistic minorities, rural, and migrants), programmes will need to be tailored to address diverse needs, to have direct, discernable outcomes and to provide incentive-rich experiences.

Knowledge-based programme design. Much more needs to be done in order to build the knowledge base and expertise employed in the service of literacy and adult education. Relative to other education areas, few research studies are being produced in literacy and adult education, and donor agencies have been too reluctant in their support serious evaluation studies or applied research. To move the field forward will require a greater emphasis on what works and what doesn't, as well as further support from donor agencies.

Openness to new approaches. A striking aspect of adult literacy work is its relative isolation. For the most part, literacy and adult education specialists and practitioners have little contact with mainstream specialists in education, and even less with sectors outside of education. There is an overall need to be open to diversity in learners and in the contexts in which they reside. No new approach is more obvious than technology, which has been taken up increasingly in the formal school settings, but has yet to have a serious input into adult education in most countries. Indeed, in developing countries, the overall limitations in fiscal and human resources have meant that technology remains far from being implemented, even though substantial cost-effectiveness appears to be achievable.

7. Conclusions

At the Jomtien conference, the literacy goal was to reduce the illiteracy rate in each country by 50 per cent in one decade. This has not happened in any country. And yet there is a widening recognition that low-literacy and poor basic learning competencies (by varying standards) are even more prevalent today than had been assumed a decade ago. Furthermore, with population growth the absolute number of illiterates has declined very little since Jomtien.

With national economies and civic participation more dependent than ever on an educated and literate citizenry, the world education community is faced with multiple and serious challenges. On the one hand, agencies which support or engage in literacy work need to be more realistic about what can be achieved within budget constraints. Such realism entails lowering expectations about major changes in individual, social and economic outcomes, while at the same time holding literacy-service providers to higher standards of accountability and professionalism. As in formal schooling, literacy and adult education do not provide a magic answer for any society, but they are part and parcel of all aspects of national development. On the other hand, agencies can enhance adult literacy programmes by:

- building a more solid knowledge base for field-based innovations,
- improving professional development and human resources capacity.
- providing better pathways from non-formal youth and adult literacy programmes into the formal school system.
- combining non-formal programmes for adults and early childhood programmes,
- taking advantage of new technologies, and

- investing resources in assessment, evaluation and monitoring, surveys and applied research, and
- creating new synergies and collaborations between governmental and non-governmental agencies.

This global thematic study has attempted to highlight some of the most important problems and prospects in improving the quality of literacy and adult education work, and efforts to meet the needs of people who are often excluded or marginalised from quality education. The importance of literacy and basic learning competencies in the lives of people the world over is difficult to overestimate. The simple fact that even today nearly one-quarter of humanity lacks such essential—and obtainable—competencies still shocks the world. It will be all the more striking in the year 2020, if we have been unable to substantially improve this situation. Yet the tools for making major gains are within reach if the best know-how can be put into service. Future literacy and adult education work will require a sustained, coherent, informed and increased effort.

◆◆◆

12

Renewed Hope: Non-Governmental Organisations and Civil Society in Education for All

1. NGOs and the unfinished agenda of EFA

Education has to be reaffirmed as a human right. As such it has to be democratised, putting emphasis on the gender issues at all levels. It has to allow every citizen (including all age groups) and every community to learn in order to develop self-confidence, participate in all democratic and development processes, take an active role in the information society and better locate themselves in the process of globalisation.

Synergies between formal and non-formal education have to be created with a focus on transforming current education systems and laying the foundations for lifelong learning for all.

Non-governmental organisations and civil society organisations have developed large networks of partnership at local, national, regional and international levels to achieve their objectives more efficiently and successfully. Partnership building has become one of their major strategies.

These are some of the conclusions reached by these organisations after an exhaustive assessment of their EFA programme.

NGOs on the move for EFA

Under the auspices of the UNESCO-NGO Collective Consultation on Literacy and Education For All, non-governmental organisations and civil society organisations engaged in the EFA 2000 Assessment undertook in-depth case studies of their own EFA programme in over fifty countries worldwide and organised national consultations in twenty-five countries of the South. Teachers also actively participated. Education International, the teachers' international union, contributed a 100-page report based on responses from teachers' unions in Bangladesh, Brazil, China, Egypt, India, Indonesia, Mexico, Nigeria and Pakistan. This impressive and participatory assessment exercise culminated in regional non-governmental organisations' consultations in Johannesburg (December1999) and Bangkok (January 2000) as well as side meetings at the Regional EFA Conferences in Cairo (January 2000) and Santo Domingo (February 2000). These meetings brought together some 200 non-governmental organisations including international, regional and national organisations, networks and coalitions. The meetings enabled non-governmental organisations to elaborate collective statements, which informed the respective Regional EFA Conferences.

National and global education campaigns, spearheaded by non-governmental organisations, aim at ensuring that the next EFA stocktaking will give the world cause to celebrate the effective achievement of the goal of Quality Education For All. These campaigns, coming on top of a massive global mobilisation of non-governmental organisations around the EFA 2000 Assessment, provide proof that educational non-governmental organisations and other civil society organisations have come of age. Non-governmental organisations have developed advocacy clout, they have sustained commitment in reaching the excluded and they have mobilised for the paradigm shift from schooling to learning. They have contributed to the conceptual development of education for the twenty-first century. Henceforth, non-governmental organisations and other civil society organisations should be supported and included at all levels of education policy-making, implementation and evaluation, if the new hope for EFA 2015 is not to become a lost opportunity.

This is the message that runs through the synthesis of the thematic reports and case studies undertaken by non-governmental organisations and other civil society organisations to complement the global EFA 2000 Assessment.

Objectives of the thematic study

This synthesis focuses specifically on three issues:

1. It analyses the activities of non-governmental organisations and civil society organisations not only from a quantitative but particularly from a qualitative perspective, paying tribute to their diversity and relating their work to the overall perspectives and trends in the international education community.
2. It examines major areas in basic education for development that have been chosen as priority areas of the in basic education for development evaluation, and describe the comparative advantages of non governmental organisations and civil society in these areas.
3. It formulates some challenges and recommendations to improve the overall context for the participation of non-governmental organisations and civil society organisations in the efforts to move towards lifelong learning for all.

Priority areas of non-governmental organisations' work

The following six priority areas were identified at the 1998 General Assembly of the NGO Collective Consultation on Literacy and Education for All. Six non-governmental organisations volunteered to co-ordinate the elaboration of individual case studies and prepare thematic synthesis (Action Aid, African Community Education Network, Education International, Asia Pacific Bureau for Adult Education, SIL International and World Education). A seventh synthesis was prepared to summarise the outcomes of national non-governmental organisations' consultations held in twenty-five countries (ActionAid). These thematic syntheses reflect important aspects of non-governmental organisations' comparative advantage in the field of education:

a) **Action Aid**: Community participation: experiences of non-governmental organisations and Civil Society;

b) **African Community Education Network**: Gender dimensions in Education for All: non-governmental organisation and civil society organisation experiences;

c) **World Education**: Linking non-formal education to development: non-governmental organisation experiences during the EFA decade;

d) **Asia Pacific Bureau for Adult Education**: Emerging trends in adult literacy policies and practice in Africa and Asia;

e) **SIL International**: Assessing civil society partnerships in EFA;

f) **Education International**: Education for All: teachers' perspectives;

g) **Action Aid**: Civil society perspectives on Education for All: broken promises, new hopes

2. Non-governmental and civil society organisations in EFA: Vision and Action

Of the various actors involved in education, including governments, the private sector, the religious community, non-governmental and civil society organisations, non-governmental organisations have particularly distinguished themselves by their efforts in non-formal education and in broadening learning experiences beyond the classroom and curriculum.

Education yes, but what kind?

All non-governmental organisations insist not only that education is a human right, but also that it has to be meaningful, relevant and of good quality. The educational objectives of non-governmental and civil society organisations are closely linked to sustainable development of the learner's milieu. This concept of education aims at developing "all individuals" and "all dimensions of a person" while also considering more functional aspects. It moves away from the classic framework of formal education to integrate all aspects of non-formal education. Whether formal or non-formal, non-governmental organisations are concerned with adapting education to the needs to the learners and their historic, socio-cultural and economic context. The fact that they are close to the grassroots and flexible in their approaches has allowed non-governmental organisations to propose 'tailor made' education, thus giving proof that alternative approaches to the formal education system are a serious and valid option, in places already a reality.

Who are all?

EFA efforts have so far not succeeded in being inclusive. Behind the overall increase in primary-school enrolment and literacy rates, there are still significant gender disparities. Disparities are also particularly significant between rural and urban areas, richer and poorer people, girls/women and boys/men or between groups of different ethnic/cultural background. Some groups have no viable access to educational opportunities, others stay outside the formal system because available education does not correspond to their learning needs and expectations. Even in the case of an expansion of the existing education systems, these different individuals and groups would continue to be excluded. The language issue is strong factor in denying access to education with minority languages being marginalised. Non-governmental organisations have the comparative advantage that they work with all different groups of learners. On all continents, in all countries, children of primary-school age (including street children and orphans), girls and women, people suffering from health problems or disabilities or people affected by war are among those who benefit from non-governmental organisation's activity. Geographically this activity is concentrated more in the South than in the North.

Non-governmental organisations have managed to give a more inclusive meaning to the world 'all' with regard to education. Even if their activities take place at the margins of mainstream education and society, they succeeded in bringing into the education movement significant groups of learners around the world, which otherwise would have not been the case.

Education for All by whom?

Non-governmental and civil society organisations have developed large networks of partnership, not only among themselves, but also with governments and other actors. Partnership-building is at the heart of non-governmental organisations work in education and is essential for improving the effectiveness and relevance of educational opportunities. The different stakeholders, including the communities, are asked to contribute to education according to their means, competence and opportunities. Non-governmental organisations organised campaigns, formed pressure groups and lobbied for debt cancellation and increases in education spending at the level of governments and financing agencies. Non-governmental and civil society organisations succeeded in mobilising communities to get involved not only as beneficiaries, but also as active agents in promoting education for all. From this perspective non-governmental organisations have clearly shown that education for all is done by all.

3. NGO Action: Diversity and scope

Community participation and the creation of a positive learning environment

Beyond education provision in schools or centres, non-governmental organisations concentrate their work on gaining a better understanding of the learning needs in a community and the creation of a positive environment for education activities. They conduct studies of the milieu, engage in social and financial mobilisation for education, develop learning materials and organise activities to alleviate the work load of women in order for them and their children to have the time and energy to participate in education programmes. Working with the communities allows non-governmental organisations to identify the use and benefit of education in that particular context. They train the different actors involved in education at local level such as teacher/parent associations, women's groups, teachers and trainers, and organise the establishment of the necessary infrastructure. Most of these activities continue, once the formal and non-formal education activities start, since they are crucial in determining their success.

Relevant content and approaches

Most non-governmental organisations give particular attention to linking educational content to the learning needs of the learners and their contexts. This requires action-research, innovations in education and, in some cases, collaboration with other development sectors and the integration of issues often neglected or absent from education programmes, such as reproductive health and HIV/AIDS, the environment, democracy and citizenship, cultural and artistic activities or new technologies.

Lifelong learning

Non-governmental organisations activities show that education begins with the young child and continues throughout

life. Activities beyond the classroom (school or centre) focus on applying and further developing what has been learned. Post-literacy activities, the creation of literate environments, training for local institutional development, youth programmes and income-generation programmes are just some examples. Non-governmental organisations also share information about their innovations and experiences within the context of national, regional and international conferences with other non-governmental organisations and with other stakeholders, including ministries and technical and financial partners.

The contribution of non-governmental organisations to EFA has been considerable

The impact of NGO activities become apparent particularly through a qualitative analysis of their action research and innovations, and leads to conclusions on improving and transforming current education systems. The fact that non-governmental organisations activity increasingly gains the attention and consideration of decision-makers and experts at national and international levels, particularly, with regard to questions of equity, relevance and quality, reflects the impact of non-governmental organisations' involvement in EFA. The thematic study concentrates on qualitative aspects, although some quantitative indication (the number of individuals and groups educated through non-governmental organisations formal and non-formal education programmes, for instance) are given. It must be noted that for a large part, these are learners who otherwise would not have had any access to education programmes.

... and it is possible to go beyond what has been achieved.

National and regional non-governmental organisations' Consultations and campaigns provided the non-governmental organisation community with a platform to make their views known and present the findings of sectoral surveys and studies, but above all to make forecasts and devise recommendations for future action. They raised important questions, which will need further reflection and follow-up:

Learning challenges for non-governmental organisations

Non-governmental and civil society organisations need to maintain a constructive, self-critical stance.

- Capacity-building for Non-governmental and civil society organisations at national and sub-regional levels will continue to be a major challenge in order for them to further strengthen their institutional and technical competencies, learn from one another and advance their collective learning.
- A deep understanding of the national policy context and global dynamics will be an important precondition in strengthening collaborative approaches in providing learning opportunities for development.
- Acknowledging and building on the diversities of non-governmental organisations will reinforce their networking.

Toward mechanisms for EFA partnership and follow-up

The Assessment has shown that improved partnership among non-governmental organisations' figure on the agenda of "renewed hope". Non-governmental organisations see themselves as partners involved at all stages of education policy and programme formulation, implementation and evaluation. As other partners acknowledge their crucial role, they will co-operate at national and international levels. In this partnership with other education stakeholders, non-governmental organisations will particularly commit themselves to areas where their comparative advantage is most significant. Lobbying for democratisation of education will continue to be an important task for non-governmental and civil society organisations.

The Draft Framework for Action on Education for All also takes up the issue of civil society involvement, but the reflection on how to best improve partnerships and create new alliances has to continue at the World Education Forum in Dakar and beyond:

- How can a systematic participation of civil society institutions in the formulation of national education policy be institutionalised at local and national level?
- How can consultative mechanisms among civil society institutions as well as between them and other partners in education be institutionalised and reinforced at all levels (international, regional, sub-regional and national)?
- How can the exchange of experience and expertise among non-governmental organisations as well as between them and other partners be reinforced at different geographical and institutional levels?

Non-governmental organisations will hold an International Consultation of non-governmental organisations prior to the World Education Forum to prepare their collective input to EFA for the future. Non-governmental organisations are prepared to strengthen partnerships with others to promote the transformation of current education systems to lay the foundations for lifelong learning for all.

◆◆◆

13

School Health and Nutrition

1. Introduction: The link between health and learning

In March 1990, world leaders gathered in Jomtien, Thailand, for the World Conference on Education for All: Meeting Basic Learning Needs. Rather than focus on the traditional issues of how to provide school buildings, textbooks and teachers, they decided instead to address the process of learning and the needs of learners. Health and nutrition were included as important contributors to the success of the learner and the learning process. This study reviews the major activities that have taken place in the school health and nutrition field around the world since Jomtien and suggests actions for the decade to come.

As numerous studies shows, education and health are inseparable: Nutritional deficiencies, helminth infections and malaria affect school participation and learning. Violence, unintentional injuries, suicidal tendencies and related lifestyle behaviours, such as the use of alcohol and other drugs, interfere with the learning process. Sexual behaviours, especially unprotected sex that results in HIV infection, other sexually transmitted diseases and unwanted or too-early pregnancies affects students' and teachers' participation in education. Importantly, many of these issues can be addressed effectively through health, hygiene, and nutrition policies and programmes for students and staff.

The information presented in this study is essential to policy—and decision-makers who are committed to achieving EFA, because the link between learning and health clearly shows that EFA is unlikely to be achieved without significant improvements in the health of students and teachers.

2. Research highlights from the past decade: what strategies are effective?

Since Jomtien, a significant amount of research has been conducted concerning the effectiveness of school health interventions, and the interrelationship among health, cognition, school participation, and academic achievement. Experience has shown that if the quality and quantity of school health programmes are to increase, the education sector must take a lead role.

Ten major findings offer important guidance for future action. School-based nutrition interventions improve academic performance. Health and nutrition status affect enrollment, retention and absenteeism. Education benefits health. Education can reduce social and gender inequities. Health promotion for teachers benefits their health, morale, and quality of instruction. Health promotion and disease prevention programmes can reduce health care costs. Treating youngsters in school can reduce disease in the community. Multiple, coordinated strategies produce a greater effect than individual strategies, but multiple strategies for any one audience must be selective and targeted. Health education is most effective when using interactive methods in a skills-based approach. Trained teachers produce more significant outcomes in student health knowledge and skills than untrained teachers.

3. Looking forward: suggestions for EFA 2015

The forthcoming decade promises great progress in strengthening the links between health and education. Major suggestions are offered for the future which emphasise the development of a shared vision, a commitment to act, a pledge to work collaboratively and the importance of a global efforts to share and acquire information. The suggestions are : First, major players in the field must join together around a common framework, relevant to the education sector. Second, to the successful, school health and nutrition efforts must be led by educators and made an integral part of efforts to improve education through educational policies and goals. Third, we must continue to deepen and expand collaboration, especially between the eduction and health sectors with mechanisms that sustain and nurture joint planning, action and learning together over time. Fourth, more investment is needed in health services for children and adolescents that they can reach easily, without stigma. Fifth, access to information as well as sustained support to use it (e.g. professional development, technical co-operation and mentoring) must be improved. Sixth, multiple targeted and co-ordinated strategies are needed to improve desired behavior patterns and health outcomes. Seventh, indicators that provide universal measures of progress are needed to focus efforts and change what is possible to report by 2015. Eight, because countries vary in terms of what they can afford, model programmes should be developed for differing levels of investment.

4. Looking back: the status of school health leading to Jomtien

International collaboration in school health has a history of more than 120 years. As the 1980s came to a close, researchers around the world were launching studies to evaluate the effectiveness of specific health interventions to address nutritional deficiencies and treatment of intestinal worms, in particular, and where possible to examine the relationship of health interventions on cognition, school attendance and other factors related to learning.

School health efforts in 1990 can be characterised in the following ways: (1) health initiatives in schools focused primarily on disease prevention; (2) confusion about the concept and definition of school health; (3) single, unco-ordinated intervention strategies; (4) few, formal mechanisms for multi-sectoral collaboration in place; (5) didactic, topic by topic teaching was a typical approach to health education; (6) evidence of effectiveness of interventions not well known or disseminated; (7) few available tools to guide assessment and strategic planning; and (8) few donors earmarking school health programmes as a priority for funding.

5. Conceptual frameworks: the principles that drive action

Since the World Conference on Education for All, a major accomplishment has been the development of conceptual framework or unifying principles to guide school health policies and programmes.

Several major frameworks have contributed to the advancement of school health and nutrition programmes. Frameworks developed in the 1990s include: the concept of the Health Promoting School (stimulated by the Ottawa Charter, 1986, and advanced by the Council of Europe, the Commission of the European Communities and WHO/European office and WHO headquarters): the Child-Friendly School (UNICEF); Basic Cost-Effective Package of School-based Interventions (World Bank and the Partnerships for Child Development, University of Oxford); and Active Learning Capacity (Levinger, EDC. for United States Agency for International Development and United Nations Development Programme).

As the decade draws to a close, some of the major players at the world level are coming together to discuss how they might build on the frameworks since Jomtien and unite around a common framework for school health. WHO, UNICEF, UNESCO and the World Bank are developing a partnership to Focus Resources on Effective School Health (FRESH), with the aim of launching this concertedly agreed upon framework at the World Eduction Forum in Senegal, April 2000. The four components of the Fresh framework are: 1) Health-related policies in schools. 2) Provision of safe water and sanitation facilities. 3) Skills-based health education. 4) School-based health and nutrition services. These components are intended to be supported by effective partnerships between teachers and health workers, effective community partnerships and pupil awareness and participation.

6. Major global trends: developments since Jomtien?

Several major global trends over the past decade have dramatically influenced the scope and direction of school health work. The AIDS pandemic stimulated new demand and urgency for school health. There was a gradual move from individual to multiple strategies and to integrated/co-ordinated approaches to health education. New mechanisms for multi-sectoral collaboration have emerged. Student and community participation have been important factors to advance school health. Skills-based methods for health education have gained recognition and greater use. Documentation and dissemination of evidence of effectiveness have increased. New tools for assessment, planning and monitoring have been piloted. Donor recognition of and investment in the filed have increased. International conferences addressed school health. Various barriers still exist that can hinder progress toward effective and sustained school health and nutrition interventions.

◆◆◆

14

Textbooks and Learning Materials 1990-99: A Global Survey

The standard of textbook provision deteriorated during the 1970s and 1980s throughout Africa and much of Latin America and Asia, and in 1990 was far below the desirable ratio of one book per pupil. Supplementary reading and other learning materials were even scarcer, and quality was often poor.

During the 1990s the situation improved in some countries, thanks in large measure to external funding by international agencies, governments and civil society organisations, but globally textbooks continued in short supply. Textbooks were particularly scarce in rural areas and, even where available, were not always used effectively. State dominance in textbook provision proved inefficient and uneconomic. Supply of learning materials was impeded by lack of funding, conflicting government priorities, difficulties in distribution and lack of trained personnel. The provision of textbooks in many countries still depended on cyclical infusions of external aid that concentrated on production of a commodity without building there related infrastructures.

Three significant trends can be detected in textbook provision during the 1990s: decentralisation of selection and procurement; economic liberalisation with a greater role for the private sector; and increased cost recovery to achieve systemic sustainability. Funding agencies sought to co-ordinate their activities and increasingly recognised the importance of developing a national publishing industry to produce textbooks that would be in stead(y supply and would reflect local conditions, experiences, and needs. In the latter part of the decade the focus of aid began to shift from supply-side provision of textbook producers to targeted subsidies and demand-side funding users.

A sustainable and competitive system of providing textbooks and other learning materials requires a publishing industry that can originate, produce and deliver the materials along commercial principles of cost recovery. Inequities will results, which can be reduced through targeted subsidies and programmes of demand-side support.

But textbooks are only part of the picture. Provision of the wide range of other books needed to foster and maintain a literate society is also contingent on the emergence of a viable publishing and bookselling industry. This goal will be beyond the capacity of many small and poor countries. Dependence on external assistance will continue, although it can be reduced through national policies of coast recovery and increased educational budgets. Electronic options, in the near—and mid-term, are unaffordable and impracticable of many regions of the world, where the problem of inequitable access to appropriate, low-cost reading material must still be addressed.

◆◆◆